Paradise Remade

Paradise Remade

The Politics of
Culture and History
in Hawai'i

ELIZABETH BUCK

Temple University Press
Philadelphia

Temple University Press, Philadelphia 19122
Copyright © 1993 by Temple University. All rights reserved
Published 1993
Printed in the United States of America

Page 31: The *Kumulipo*, from Martha W. Beckwith, trans. and ed., *The
Kumulipo: A Hawaiian Creation Chant* (Honolulu: University of Hawaii
Press, 1972), 58, 187, copyright © the University of Hawaii Press, is used by
permission of the University of Hawaii Press.

Pages 115–116: "Kaulana Nā Pua," from *Na Mele O Hawai'i Nei*, collected
by Samuel H. Elbert and Noelani Mahoe (Honolulu: University of Hawaii
Press, 1970), 62–64, copyright © the University of Hawaii Press, is used by
permission of the University of Hawaii Press.

Page 117: The campaign chant of William Kaho'owaiwai Kāma'u, from
Eleanor Williamson, "Hawaiian Chants and Songs Used in Political
Campaigns," in *Directions in Pacific Traditional Literature*, ed. Adrienne L.
Kaeppler and H. Arlo Nimmo (Honolulu: Bishop Museum Press, 1976),
137–138, is used by permission of the Bishop Museum Press.

Pages 177–178: "Fish and *Poi*," by Eaton Magoon, Jr., is used by permission
of Bob Magoon.

Cover photo: Art Direction—Alton Brecker
           Photography—Ric Noyle
           Photographed for Altillo's European Menswear
           Dancers—Alvin Hanzawa, Rand Stewart, Michael Casupang

Library of Congress Cataloging-in-Publication Data
Buck, Elizabeth Bentzel.
    Paradise remade : the politics of culture and history in Hawai'i /
Elizabeth Buck.
      p. cm.
    Includes bibliographical references (p.   ) and index.
    ISBN 0-87722-978-3
    1. Hawaiians—Social life and customs.   2. Hawaiians—History.
    3. Acculturation—Case studies.   4. Hula (Dance)   5. Hawaii—
Historiography.   I. Title.
    DU624.65.B83   1993
    996.9—dc20   92-310

In memory of Bill

Contents

Paradise Remade

combining elements of show business, sex, comedy, and "cultural education." It all adds up to the dominant tourist-industry myth of Hawai'i as an accessible paradise, one that promises and delivers more than beautiful beaches and balmy weather—"more" being the human element of a culture and the "*aloha* spirit" that make Hawai'i something special.

The show-business practices give the Kodak Hula Show its form and dynamic. It is present in the role of the emcee who moves the show along, signaling the start of one segment ("Let's welcome our Tahitian dancers") or the end of another ("Let's give a round of applause for our dancing girls"). Above all, the show-business element is there in the way Hawaiian culture is framed and positioned for an observing audience, in the regularity of its performance (four days a week for more than fifty years), in the souvenir stands at the entrance, in the totality of the production that transforms ancient rituals into an exotic show for the consumption of tourists. Show business is also there in the comic and sexual elements, which alter the pace of the slower *hula*, enlivening what might otherwise bore the uninformed audience. A comic element is injected as older women, the *tūtū wāhine*, in their long *mu'umu'u* dance a funny, naughty *hula*, while the emcee alludes to the ancient *hula ma'i* that symbolized in body movements the procreative powers of the chiefly *ali'i*. Thus the Hawaiian celebration of the body in the ancient *hula* is reduced to sexual innuendoes for comic relief. The more exotic and erotic part of the show comes in the brief presentation of Tahitian dance and dancers: "Let's go to Tahiti." The shimmying young dancers are told to "take it right to them. Let's get a close-up." This segment drops any pretense of education, focusing the gaze on the rapidly moving hips, bare midriffs, and bra-covered breasts, all moving to the intense beat of Tahitian drumming in the background.

The gloss of education comes next, in the explanations (greatly simplified) of how Hawaiian culture used to be: "Today you'll learn about the history of the *hula*, its styles, and what the movements of the dances mean." As the "*hula* girls" demonstrate, the audience is told what the different hand movements represent: the sun and moon, the stars, and the winds. In another "educational" segment a Hawaiian man (perhaps it is King Kali transformed by the magic of show business from *ali'i* to *maka'āinana* (commoner), flanked by *hula* girls for added visual effect, demonstrates how *poi* is made by pounding *taro*. The man and the women pose three times in this tableau, in front of each section of the tourist-filled bleachers, so that everyone in the crowd can capture the scene on film.[4] The emcee tells the audience, "This is the way they did it back in the old days."

The history of the islands is narrated as the changing forms and styles of *hula* are performed in rapid succession, from ancient *hula kahiko* to twentieth-century *hapa haole hula*, but it is a confusing history. Intermixed and equally weighted are random references to King Kalākaua, Queen Lili'uokalani on her throne, the coming of the missionaries and their insistence on the body-covering *mu'umu'u*, the opening of the Royal Hawaiian Hotel in 1927, statehood, the *'ukulele* and guitar-playing cowboys. This narrative of historical events and people is abbreviated, and its silences are significant. Unspoken is why and how it is that the ancient *hula* now coexists with a *hula* danced to a song like "The Cockeyed Mayor of Kaunakakai," or why the referred-to monarchy of King Kalākaua and Queen Lili'uokalani (represented in the royal creation of the Kodak Hula Show—King Kali) no longer exists.

In addition to the Kodak Hula Show, dinner shows in Waikīkī hotels feature the same kind of tourist-packaged Hawaiian–Polynesian music. These shows, which accompany *lū'au* on hotel grounds or are performed in large hotel showrooms, are even more slickly packaged than the Kodak Hula Show, and the audiences pay handsomely to be entertained. In the smaller hotel lounges, however, one is sometimes lucky enough to find performers of Hawaiian music that runs the gamut from long-familiar *hapa haole* music to rock, pop, and reggae-inspired contemporary Hawaiian music. These musicians draw local residents to Waikīkī or the few nightspots in other parts of Honolulu where performers such as the Peter Moon Band, Eddie Kamae and the Sons of Hawaii, and Olomana get brief bookings to perform for appreciative local audiences, Hawaiian and non-Hawaiian. Throughout the year, there are also events (fund raisers, family *lūʻau*, festivals, songfests, chant and *hula* competitions) in which Hawaiian musicians, singers, and dancers (some of the same ones who entertain in Waikīkī) perform for people who understand and love Hawaiian music.

Competing Myths of Hawaiʻi

Hawaiian music is many things, used many ways, serving different histories and myths of Hawaiʻi. The now-dominant myth of Hawaiʻi appropriates Hawaiian music as a signifier of a tourist paradise. The alternative myth, the one projected by Hawaiians seeking to regain their history, identity, and sovereignty, reappropriates Hawaiian music. Here it becomes a signifier of a society that before contact with the West was complex and elaborate, of a history of destruction and domination after contact, and of a people attempting to challenge the structures of power in late-twentieth-century Hawaiʻi.

All myths distort the past and the present. The ideological work of any dominant myth is to make itself look neutral and innocent and, in the process, to naturalize human relationships of power and domination.[5] This is what the dominant myth of Hawaiʻi as paradise does so well. It appropriates Hawaiian culture and forms of representation, including Hawaiian music, to its ideological tasks, in the process transforming old meanings into new ones.

The dominant myth is evident in the ways that the forms of Hawaiian music, particularly chant and *hula*, are used as representations of Hawaiʻi as a paradise for tourists, something to be seen and enjoyed without wondering about the past or its meaning to Hawaiian performers—those who appear to have created their dances with a view to exotic festivity for foreign consumption.[6] The dominant myth of paradise prefers to work with simple styles of *hula*—with happy *hapa haole hula*—not with the complex range of chant and *hula*. In these reconstituted and simplified forms, chant and *hula* trivialize the history of the islands. Their original meanings are obscured, and new signification is given by the myth of paradise.

> In passing from history to nature, myth acts economically: it abolishes the complexity of human acts, it gives them the simplicity of essences, it does away with all dialectics, with any going back beyond what is immediately visible, it organizes a world which is without contradictions because it is without depth, a world wide open and wallowing in the evident, it establishes a blissful clarity: things appear to mean something by themselves.[7]

The ideology of the dominant myth of Hawai'i is evident in the practices that govern performance and the codes of audience etiquette. Hawaiian *hula* is allocated to hotels and tourists, European ballet to concert halls and elite audiences. The ballet is performed to respectful silence; at hotels, *hula* is accompanied by the audience's consumption of *lomi lomi* salmon, *poi*, pork, Mai Tais, Blue Hawaiis, Chi Chis, all of them—food, drink, dance, and music—served up as signifiers of paradise. That these distinctions between *hula* and ballet are taken for granted is a product of the dominant myth, which makes these practices appear natural when they are in fact tied to a particular ideological definition of reality. Where chant and *hula* are heard and seen in contexts of cultural consumption, they have spatial presence but are deprived of memory.

But not all *hula* is performed for tourists in Waikīkī and on the neighbor islands. Major events throughout the year are the focus of attention for the serious practitioners of chant and *hula* and their public. Since the 1970s, with the so-called Hawaiian Renaissance, many Hawaiians have become intensely interested in learning ancient and more modern styles of *hula*. *Hula hālau* (schools) organized in the 1970s, as well as long-established ones, have been filled by young Hawaiians who want to learn about Hawaiian culture and history; chant and *hula* offer a way to that end. *Hālau* have given Hawaiians a place to learn about their culture and thus about themselves, and to grasp the complexity and beauty of the Hawaiian language and the dynamic history of Hawai'i before Western contact. Joining a *hālau* and working hard to learn and perform *hula* are statements of individual and community identity. In effect, *hālau* have played an important role in the politicization of culture in Hawai'i. By giving structure, place, and meaning for Hawaiian cultural practices, they are part of contemporary ethnopolitics.

Over the past two decades, *hula* and chant have been a microcosm of the cultural politics of the islands. The competing myths and histories of Hawai'i are waged in the practice and performance of *hula* and chant. Not only is there the obvious division between Waikīkī *hula* and *hālau hula,* one performed for the uninformed and the other for the aficionado of the forms and meaning of *hula,* but even within the latter, there are intense debates about tradition, authenticity, and legitimacy. For many *kumu hula* and their students, chant and *hula* are sacred legacies from the past that must be preserved and protected. For others, chant and *hula* offer opportunities for creativity. These debates most often arise at the big annual competition of the Merrie Monarch Festival. All involved—dancers, *kumu hula,* judges, audience—watch with the sharp eyes of critics and criticize with equally sharp tongues.

One of the winningest *kumu hula,* Johnny Lum Ho, has frequently been reproached for deviating from established steps and moves of the ancient *hula.* Other *kumu hula* have also been criticized for being too innovative with *hula* movements, with costuming, or with general presentation. One of the most respected of the traditional *kumu hula,* Noenoelani Zuttermeister, says: "Each thing has to work hand in hand. It wouldn't make sense any other way. If I took a traditional chant and I put a rock 'n' roll step in there, would you call that kahiko? No, because the steps are not kahiko. Or say I do everything traditional—I get the feet right, I get the hands right, I get the chant right—and I dress the dancer in a cellophane skirt. It wouldn't make sense."[8] Wendell P. K. Silva, in the introduction to a 1984 book on practicing *kumu hula*, says the following:

> Hawai'i is indeed fortunate that remnants of this ancient hula have been passed on to our time. However, the remaining vestiges of this hula are relatively few and represent a precious legacy for all of us. Hula resources who possess this cherished gift, guard it well and are justifiably selective in its sharing. Not only are these people entrusted with valuable hula knowledge of Hawai'i's hula past, they are charged with the responsibility of preserving these hulas in a pure and unadulterated form. . . . These hula resources subscribe to the belief that to preserve is to perpetuate the hula.
>
> Concurrent with this belief, there are those in the teaching community who advocate the dynamism of the hula kahiko. . . . Proponents of this school of thought credit exciting and innovative interpretations of the hula kahiko as an important factor in stimulating the rejuvenation of interest in hula as it is performed at present.[9]

Kalena Silva, another Hawaiian scholar, makes the following distinctions between what is acceptable and what is not:

> The kinds of changes that came about among people who still spoke Hawaiian as their first language, whose cultural base was still Hawaiian, to me are generally acceptable. But many of the changes we are seeing today in hula are basically from among people whose first language is English, whose cultural base is a local culture which is very mixed and heavily Western. So from that background, these people are creating things that are very foreign.[10]

Debates over what should and should not be done to *hula* will no doubt continue as long as *hula* is performed. The intense feelings that Hawaiians involved in *hula* bring to its practice and performance are indicative of the meanings these cultural forms hold for contemporary Hawaiians.

Before contact with the West, the meanings of chant and *hula* were inherent in the social and sacred context of their performance. When Hawai'i was penetrated by outsiders, the dances became objects of study or objects of scorn, and their meanings were impoverished. With tourism, *hula* was tamed and domesticated by the myth of paradise. In the late twentieth century, *hula* and chant have been reappropriated by Hawaiians in the settings of *hula hālau* and serious public performances.

Many Hawaiians are trying to understand the old meanings of chant and *hula* from living practitioners of Hawaiian culture or within the formal academic setting of the University of Hawaii. Says Ho'oulu Cambra, a *kumu hula* who teaches at the university: "It has always amazed me how the composers of these chants were able to combine major ideas and themes into a few concise, terse lines. You can't help but respect and admire the Hawaiian culture if you know the language and can read the chants. Hula is a way of life, it is a people's inspiration. It is the Hawaiian's connection to the universe around him."[11] At the same time that old chants are being translated and studied in the halls of academe, performed chant and *hula* are being invested with new meanings reflective of their contemporary historical and political contexts. According to one of the younger *kumu hula*, Māpuana de Silva:

We have tried to re-create the chant and dance tradition of Kailua which for several generations has largely been hidden in books and Hawaiian language newspapers. Did you know that Kawainui Marsh was once a fishpond and before that a lagoon? Did you know that Hawaiians have lived on its banks for 1500 years and that Kailua was once immeasurably wealthy and an ancient center for the arts? It's my duty and pleasure to revive the chants which speak of those things, and to create new mele that remind us of what was, describe what is, and ask of what will be.[12]

In the debates over authenticity and traditional movements, words, and dress, Hawaiians make them the objects of their expert and scholarly discourse. But in the experiential moments of performance, whether in the practice halls of the *halau* or before the expectant crowds of the Merrie Monarch or Prince Lot festivals, they are invested with collective meanings that shape a new and still emerging Hawaiian identity. Says Olana Ai, one of the younger *kumu hula:* "Finally the Hawaiians are dancing for themselves. Not just for the gods, not just for the ali'i, not just for the tourists but finally for themselves."[13] For Hawaiian performers and audiences, *hula* and chant are now the strongest cultural links to a distant and glorious past. They are vivid, public markers of Hawaiian difference and identity. To *kumu hula* John W. Keānuenue Ka'imikaua, "The hula is the inspiration that will enable the Hawaiians to rise up from the dust out of obscurity. It is the last hope that can make us feel Hawaiian and remember our culture and forefathers. The dance will thus be the last of our cultural strongholds that may well preserve our dying heritage."[14] To me, as an outsider, the *hula* and chant performances of these intense, serious, and dedicated dancers say: "*We* are Hawaiian, and this is *our* culture. It is *the* culture of the islands. Watch and be amazed!"

History and the Politics of Culture

A succession of mythopolitical representations of reality have appropriated chant and *hula* (and more recent forms of Hawaiian music) over the course of Hawaiian history from well before to long after contact with the West. Like all myths, these overlapping and sometimes contending stories are ambiguous and blurred. Each myth has inscribed chant and *hula* within its own political ideology, thus changing their practices of production and their meanings.

Much of the struggle over power in Hawai'i has taken place in the arena of culture. The politics of culture certainly did not start with Western contact, but the rules of discourse and the players in the contest were radically altered from that time on. Two hundred years after Captain James Cook's arrival, one hundred years after the American overthrow of the Hawaiian monarchy, and three decades after statehood, Hawaiians are still struggling over issues of land, sovereignty, and their identity as Hawaiians. These struggles are played out in various arenas—the courts, the legislative bodies of Congress and the state, the newspapers and broadcast media—and in front of bulldozers. In recent years, however, the politics of culture also have been waged in academic settings and journals.[15]

Increasingly, in the humanities and the social sciences (particularly in Pacific history and anthropology) long-held assumptions of what constitutes knowledge and how knowledge is produced are being challenged. Greg Dening, one of the most perceptive historians in and of the Pacific, observes how explicitly political Pacific history has become, and how liberating history can be if it is open to multiple ways of knowing and recounting it, including the vernacular histories of legends, anecdotes, plays, dance—the practices whereby people express their lives and identities in their telling of the past. Dening calls for reflective histories that are aware that "the telling is not the reality," that when people express their knowledge of the past, they are saying something about themselves and the symbolic environment of the present. "The past is never contemporary, but history always is. History is always bound to the present in some way. History always represents the present in the ways it re-presents the past."[16]

Some historians recognize that theory (some internal model of interpretation) is unavoidable; that the selection and foregrounding of certain past events, people, and forces and the silencing of others is the product of contemporary cultural codes; and that historians' distinctions between direct and indirect observation, between primary and secondary data overshadow more basic questions about the construction of meanings.

Fernand Braudel, one of the leaders of the *Annales* school, distinguishes between three kinds of histories: the traditional histories of events, or "microhistory," where "events cling to each other" and "great men appear regularly organizing things"; the histories of conjunctures that examine major social and material "expansions and contractions"; and structural histories of the *longue durée* that "inquire into whole centuries at a time," considering the "inexhaustible history of structures and groups of structures."[17] Traditional/empiricist histories discourage theory and philosophy, privileging observational facts or data, focusing on documentary evidence and reliability of sources. The accepted notion that the past can be retrieved and accurately recounted fails to recognize that the data of history, even the privileged "primary" sources, were inscribed by ideologies that informed the perceptions of eyewitness observers and social commentators. All accounts, even first-person accounts, are representations of reality, not reality itself, and therefore are always selective along socially constituted lines of what is worthy or not worthy of note.

We need to take into account the possibility that our contact with the past will always pass through the imaginary and through its ideologies, will always in one way or another be mediated by the codes and motifs of some deeper historical classification system or *pensee sauvage* of the historical imagination, some properly political unconscious.[18]

Narrative historiography, because it is a storytelling form, emphasizes the human character of history, placing individual, personal reasons for action, rather than impersonal forces of structure, at the center. Traditional narrative histories are more concerned with an accurate recounting of the temporal sequence of events than explaining *why* societies work as they do or the reasons behind geopolitical transitions that occur over the *longue durée*. Although narrative is apparently natural to the way we speak about the world and events in it, the forms, conventions, and styles of historical narrative are socially constituted in ways that mark certain events, people, and forces as noteworthy and marginalizing others.[19] Thus the practices of historiography are never innocent because they construct meaning out of the past that either reinforces or challenges contemporary social relationships.

Hawaiian Historiography

Most histories of Hawai'i written in the twentieth century weave a continuing story out of the major events of the documented past and the deeds or misdeeds of major figures on the historical scene. The events related are those that possess the character of narrativity, that seemingly tell themselves, that appear to be incontrovertibly important and "real." Often these histories of Hawai'i begin their chronological narratives with Captain Cook's arrival. The selection of this event of Western discovery as the narrative beginning of Hawaiian history reflects not only one of the dominant epistemological assumptions of modern historiography but also Western views of non-Western civilizations, particularly those that have been incorporated into the historic destiny of the West (e.g., American Indian, African, Central and South American, and Hawaiian).

In effect, such ideological practices have compounded the effects of Western imperialism. For instance, a major assumption that has played an important role in Hawaiian historiography is that history proper begins with writing, that what precedes documentable history is "prehistory," perceived by historians trained in positivist schools of historiography as a dubious combination of myth and fact and therefore highly problematic for narratives that aim to produce an "accurate" account of past reality. Consequently, most of the published and taught accounts of the pasts of Third World cultures, including Hawai'i, have been written by Westerners based on Western observations and interpretations, a situation that has had significant implications for relationships of power.

The Western distinction between prehistory and history, particularly when applied to an oral culture such as existed in Hawai'i, intersects with the introduction of writing and the imposition of English as the dominant language of knowledge, becoming part of the total package of Western political, economic, and cultural domination. To the extent that mainstream histories of Hawai'i bring "precontact" Hawai'i (another Western ethnocentric term) into their narratives, it is usually in timeless, ahistorical, anthropological descriptions of what life was like in Hawai'i before the arrival of Westerners. This is what Johannes Fabian calls "allochronic" discourse, the positioning of other cultures into a static ethnographic present, denying coevalness between the Western observer and the observed.[20] All the vast time of Hawai'i's past that was represented in its epic, poetic, and genealogical chants is silenced or relegated to the dubious (for historians) categories of folklore and myth. The history of the changing political and religious alignments of gods and humans, of heroic battles and the rise and fall of powerful ali'i, is reduced to sediments in brief prologues that talk in terms of "isolated islands that time had passed by."

What then follows in these histories are narratives that chronicle Hawaiian history after Western great men reached Hawai'i's shores, foregrounding events and actors that, to Western observers, marked the evolution of Hawai'i from primitiveness to progressing civilization—the arrival of Captain Cook in 1778 and his demise in 1779, the unification of the islands by Kamehameha I during the late 1700s and early 1800s, the formal abolition of the kapu system in 1819 by Kamehameha II and Ka'ahumanu, the arrival of the first contingent of missionaries in 1820 (the beginning of moral order), the successive steps leading to the constitution of Western-style government (the institution of political order), the introduction of economic "reforms" and modern systems of trade and finance (the institution of economic order), the overthrow of the monarchy in 1893 (the establishment of democracy), and so on. These are histories inscribed with Western assumptions of what constitutes social progress and morality.[21] Missing from most twentieth-century accounts of the eighteenth and nineteenth centuries are the events and developments that Westerners were not privy to and that therefore could not be marked as significant to the progress of island history. Written in scientific, objective, and realistic styles with the historical narrator effaced and his or her moral impulses—conscious or unconscious—obscured, the events of Hawai'i's history after Western contact unfold in narratives that appear natural and nonrhetorical.

Most important, missing from these histories is a sense of the radical transformations (political, economic, cultural, and demographic) that were taking place in the islands. The far-reaching structural changes initiated in the nineteenth century and that continue today are obscured in what Braudel would call the "microhistories" of Hawai'i. Certainly the transformations of social structure have been more significant for the present and future course of the islands than the individuals and events that occupy center stage in mainstream histories. These narratives usually take the literary form that Kenneth Burke characterizes as "syllogistic progression." The narratives make events appear as part of a pattern, an inevitable cause-and-effect chain reaction proceeding with a relentless inevitability that links events so that they display, to quote Hayden White, "the coherence, integrity, fullness, and closure of an image of life that is and can only be imaginary."[22] Burke's syllogistic progression is similar to what White calls "historical emplotments," the ways in which a historian weaves a narrative prose account of the past into a story plot that may be a romance, a tragedy, a comedy or a satire.[23] Two competing emplotments of Hawaiian history are often woven together in historical accounts: one creates a drama peopled by romanticized Hawaiians and exploitative whites; the other tells of savages that have benefited from the civilizing institutions and practices of the Christian West. The emplotments of these accounts have been either what White calls "tragedies" (resignation to a lost culture and a despoiled land) or "comedies" (reconciliation of conflict through the harmony of *aloha*, economic progress, and cultural assimilation)—what might, for Hawai'i, be called the "rainbow effect."

Alternative Histories of Hawai'i

But the narrative recounting of events, people, and social trends does seem to be the natural, common-sense way of telling history. What would be the approaches and foci of alternative histories of Hawai'i? What would they select as narrative domains? For an Althusserian Marxist–informed history, the focus would be on transformations in Hawai'i's structural formations and accompanying changes in the political, ideological, and economic elements that make up the social structure. For a poststructuralist, Foucaultian-informed history of Hawai'i, the historical field would be the emergence of contending forces of discursive power as Western definitions of reality and knowledge displaced Hawaiian.

In recent years, alternative histories of Hawai'i have been published that move beyond the traditional narratives of great people and events. These include the critical histories of Noel Kent, David Stannard, and Haunani-Kay Trask;[24] the histories that foreground the *maka'āinana* (commoners) rather than the *ali'i* (chiefs) in the nineteenth century, or workers and rural and urban communities rather than economic and political leaders in the twentieth century (like those by Caroline Ralston, Edward Beechert, Ronald Takaki, and Davianna McGregor);[25] histories of the political economy of land and development in twentieth-century Hawai'i by George Cooper and Gavan Daws;[26] and anthropological analyses of the historical conjuncture when the West and Hawai'i met by Marshall Sahlins, Jocelyn Linnekin, Valerio Valeri, Alan Howard, and Robert Borofsky.[27]

In addition, scholars able to read nineteenth-century materials written in Hawaiian (such as those by Lilikāli Kame'eleihiwa, Jocelyn Linnekin, and John Charlot) are beginning to redress the bias of histories that have relied on Western narratives or descriptions or on published translations of Hawaiian accounts (including my own).[28] All these narratives and analyses (and many others not mentioned here but present in the endnotes) have informed my own interpretation of Hawaiian history. I also recognize my reliance on the histories that I have just criticized. For instance, Kuykendall's three-volume history of the monarchy period is invaluable for its marshaling of information from English-language sources of that period.

The histories informed by dependency theory (Kent's) and structural anthropology (by Sahlins and Valeri) are particularly relevant to my interpretation of the islands' history. But the questions that dependency theory and structural anthropology pose and the way they are posed are variously limiting and reductionist: dependency theory tending toward economism, structural anthropology toward idealism. Dependency theory marginalizes political, ideological, and even economic practices not involved in the encompassing economic pull of the center of the world system. Structural anthropology privileges preexisting cultural categories, thereby emphasizing the continuous over the discontinuous. "Instead of a discussion of the conditions, poetic, political and historical, in which cultural texts were constructed and performed, we get the structuralist will to resolve puzzles, to see coherency and the resolution of contradiction."[29]

A Structural Account of Hawai'i

My interpretation of Hawai'i's history focuses on that second level of history identified by Braudel—that of the conjuncture—where the trajectories of Western and Hawaiian history meet in what was a major discontinuity in the *longue durée* of Hawai'i's history. The nineteenth century was a "structural rift" for Hawai'i.[30] During that period, fundamental social relationships, cultural frameworks, long-standing political and economic practices, and hence structures of power were radically altered. In this history, I have taken concepts from various theories of social formation and change. My analysis couples Marxist-informed concepts of social formations, ideology, and forms of symbolic representation with poststructuralist conceptualizations of the power of linguistic practices and how power in terms of social relationships, knowledge, and identities are shaped by discursive regimes. It is not offered as *the* narrative of Hawaiian history but as an alternative among other recent narratives that challenge the traditional accounts of these islands.

Although this is a history of the islands and not a history of chant and *hula,* Hawaiian music and the changing historical contexts of its production, practice, and meaning offer a way of "reading" the history of Hawai'i. Using Barthes's notion of intertext,[31] I view Hawaiian music as a continuous productivity where culture, creativity, and social forces interact, creating and re-creating meaning. Long before Cook arrived, Hawaiian chant and *hula* had been changing as the economic, political, and ideological structures of the islands changed; it is still developing as each new wave of outside cultural and social influence reaches the islands and as relationships of power are reformed. By looking at the ways chant, *hula,* and contemporary Hawaiian music have been variously used and discursively constituted by different groups and institutions over time, music emerges as an important arena of struggle—a site where the "politics of culture" were engaged in the past and continue to be contested in the present.

One force in the histories of colonized people has not been adequately addressed by theories of history, politics, and culture. For Hawai'i, it was a force that was as powerful as, if not more powerful than, any of the other forms of power that served the domination of the West. More culturally devastating than capitalism and the incompatible culture of the West was the force of disease. Various estimations of the islands' population at Cook's arrival range from a low of two hundred thousand to more than eight hundred thousand. From 40 to 65 percent of Hawaiians died from diseases, including venereal diseases, measles, tuberculosis and other respiratory illnesses, within fifty years after Cook and his crew arrived in 1778. The first credible missionary count, in 1832, estimated only one hundred thirty thousand Hawaiians living in the islands. The first official census, in 1853, reported the number of Hawaiians at seventy-three thousand. In 1878, during Kalākaua's reign, there were fewer than fifty-eight thousand Hawaiians alive.[32] Certainly this physical devastation of the Hawaiian people worked in tandem with all the other forces of Western imperialism. The very rapid depopulation of the Hawaiian race during the nineteenth century raises a fundamental question for any account of the transformation of Hawaiian chant and *hula:* How does the devastation of a race affect its production and practice of music?

Hawaiian history, as any human history, eludes theoretical closure. There are no simple, single explanations of the dynamic, dialectic relationships between structure, events, people, motivations, and chance that constitute Hawai'i's past. The epistemological lesson—no less than the moral lesson, since we are speaking of Truth (or at least the power to say what is Truth)—is that all historical accounts, including my own, must be approached with an awareness of the inherent limitations of the assumptions under which their questions are formulated and, hence, their implications for legitimating (or delegitimating) existing structures of power and the various forces that seek to challenge them. With these caveats in mind, I offer my interpretation of Hawai'i's past and present.

Chapter Two

Thinking about Hawaiian History

> All science would be superfluous if the outward
> appearance and the essence of things directly coincided.
>
> Marx, *Capital*

With any history, we need to think backward, to imagine the past. But we necessarily think about the past within the ideological constructs of the present. It is difficult enough to understand our own histories; it is particularly difficult to grasp the historical experiences of non-Western cultures because we are not only constrained in our thinking by the present but by the historical experiences of the West and dominant interpretations of those experiences. In looking at Hawai'i's past, we are faced by the same problems that Marx encountered in trying to conceptualize social relations and institutions in societies in which economic, political, and ideological practices were not shaped by the forces of capitalism. We must somehow come to terms with two alternative interpretive stances: identity and difference. Identity is unreflexively seeing Hawai'i as intuitively accessible to us, and so we impose our own social categories and ways of thinking on its past structures and practices. The opposite is to project Hawai'i's past as so radically different and alien from our own that we can never comprehend it.[1] If there is an answer, it lies somewhere in the gap between the dominant imageries and ideologies of the islands' past and silence.

Conceptualizing Structural Change:
Marxist Perspectives

Applying Marxist-informed and poststructuralist theories to Hawai'i focuses attention on the formation and transformation of successive social structures, on the sites and practices of ideology within those changing structures, and on relationships of power and domination within Hawaiian society before contact with the West and between Hawai'i and the West after contact. To talk about Hawai'i's past and current social structures is not simply to note that Hawaiian society has always been complex and that everything interacts with everything else. Instead, it requires identifying determining social forces and then showing how these forces have been embedded within social practices and relationships over time.[2] A structural analysis of Hawai'i looks at how material and economic production has been organized and how resulting benefits have been socially distributed; it ascertains the various ways that political power has been allocated, held, and withheld; and it pays close attention to the ways in which ideological practices explicitly and implicitly have legitimated relationships of power and mystified social inequities.

Modes of Production

"Mode of production" was Marx's organizing concept for categorizing and analyzing social structures. In its fullest formulation, the concept of mode of production pertains to how, in a particular social formation in a given time, the totality of political, economic, and ideological practices and institutions come together, how relationships of power are reproduced, and why change occurs. In applying Marxist-informed notions of social structure and changing modes of production to Hawaiian history, I have tried to avoid the "vulgar Marxisms" of economic determinism or history-as-class-struggle narratives. Although Marx fully recognized the power of human consciousness and agency, he believed that ideas, beliefs, and values do not exist independently of the material conditions of life and human activities. The philosophical underpinning of structural Marxism, most notably as reinterpreted by Louis Althusser and other twentieth-century theorists, is the notion that there are material social structures that are not created and imposed by a subjective, collective consciousness.

Marx held that in any mode of production the material and economic aspects of life are determinant "in the last instance." Only under the capitalist mode of production, however, are economic forces dominant. In attempting to counter the economic determinism of Stalinist revisions of Marx and Engels, as well as the humanistic, subject-centered interpretations of existential Marxism, Althusser distanced and, in effect, indefinitely postponed economic determination, eliminated the notion of class conflict as the driving force of social change, and extended (but also, in the end, functionalized) Marx's concept of ideology.[3]

Following Marx, Althusser conceptualized the structure of a society as a complex whole consisting of distinct but interrelated "instances" or "levels": the economic, the political, and the ideological. A particular articulation of political, economic, and ideological forces, practices, and institutions constitutes a mode of production in any specific society at any given time in history. The dominant level of the dominant mode of production generates the overall character of a society.[4] "Mode of production," however, is an ideal categorical term because in most societies two or more modes of production coexist, with one mode dominant and others either residual from the past or anticipatory of the future. "Structural formation" was Althusser's term for capturing the totality of coexisting modes of production.

Social Reproduction and Change

What is it that gives social stability to a seemingly precarious social formation with its competing, coexisting modes of production? How does a society reproduce itself and maintain its social coherency over time? What, conversely, causes change? Why are there internally generated ruptures and breaks in social structures? What happens when extraneous forces impinge on a social structure? These are questions that a structural history of Hawai'i must attempt to answer.

Understanding reproduction—why a society stays more or less the same from generation to generation—focuses attention on

practices, beliefs, and institutions that maintain social relationships; understanding transformation—why a society changes—
focuses on processes and forces that lead to strains, ruptures, and
reformations of a society at specific historical conjunctures. In
any society, at any time, processes and forces of reproduction and
transformation are present. The ascendancy of forces of stability
over change, or vice versa, depends on many factors and circumstances. For Hawai'i, the nineteenth century was a historical conjuncture where forces of transformation far outweighed those of
reproduction.

Ideology and Social Reproduction

The interactive mediation of economic, political, and ideological practices reproduce a society over time. Social stability is primarily the province of ideology, the religious, legal–juridical, and
political systems and practices of a society that govern relationships of power along multiple dimensions of class, gender, race,
and ethnicity. Ideology is materialized in concrete practices and
rituals, evident in the "lived relations" of our day-to-day lives.
Ideology interpellates us into multiple social roles, constructing
motivations, commitments, and beliefs that we share with others
in our society. Social relations and dominant representations of
those relations preexist us. We are born into these structured
practices of ideology. Althusser's emphasis on "lived relations"
stresses the notion that ideology is continuously played out in
our daily lives. It is not manipulated by any one class, although
ideology is embedded in and reinforces the structuring lines of
power, class, and gender.[5]

All social practices materialize ideology, producing and repro-
ducing meaning. Nevertheless, certain sites are invested with
ideological "responsibility," most notably those institutions and
apparatuses that produce our shared ideas and representations
of reality,[6] including religion, education, literature, art, music,
and media—those practices and institutions whose "business"
it is to articulate definitions of morality, legitimate relation-

ships of power, and define social identities. Ideology produces social consensus, mystifying relations of domination and subordination so that they seem natural. When relations of power and domination are taken for granted, a situation of social hegemony, in the Gramscian sense, exists. When a state enjoys a situation of hegemony, existing forces and centers of authority are seen as natural even by those who are dominated and oppressed by them. Hegemony, therefore, does not imply the absence of contradictions; it is simply that relations of domination—always associated with contradiction—are accepted as part of the natural order.[7]

Hegemonic situations existed in Hawai'i prior to contact with the West and, to a large extent, a hegemonic situation exists today. But throughout the nineteenth century and the first half of the twentieth century, the social structure of the islands was undergoing such tremendous change that little of Hawaiian society appeared "natural" or unproblematic for the diverse cultural groups living in the islands. Between Hawaiians and Western colonizers there was no shared consensus of reality, and from the late nineteenth century until the 1950s there was significant social and political conflict arising from the plantation economy and the many immigrants from Asia and elsewhere.

Contradiction and Change

Within Althusserian Marxist theory, change results primarily from contradictions that are inherent to the social structure and day-to-day material conditions rather than from human agency and action. Contradictions are produced by fundamental forces and principles of the social system that "operate in terms of each other but at the same time contravene one another."[8] They result from the way a society is structured and institutionalized to reproduce itself, and they are always present when relations of domination are systemic. Hegemony does not imply the absence of contradictions, but in a hegemonic situation contradictions are contained and mystified. When, however, contradictions become too intense and too apparent to be ignored, social relationships that had been taken for granted are politicized, the social structure fractures, and change takes place. Therefore, just as stability is inscribed within the social structure, so too are the seeds of social transformation.

The already existing contradictions within the Hawaiian hierarchical social structure became apparent and politicized during the initial years of contact with the West.[9] A Marxist history of Hawai'i, therefore, identifies contradictions that were inherent in the islands' social structure, how they arose and affected fundamental social relationships, and how they were manifested at specific historical conjunctures when fundamental social changes were taking place. Before 1800, structural changes were generated primarily from within. Throughout the nineteenth century, Western imperialism and colonialism imposed a new mode of production on the islands—capitalism. The collision of vastly different social structures with radically divergent political, economic, and ideological practices resulted in a social reformation that reallocated power from Hawaiians to Westerners.

Noncapitalist Social Formations

Processes of structural reproduction and transformation differ radically in noncapitalist and capitalist societies. To understand how Marxist-informed concepts of structure, developed primarily with capitalist societies in mind, can be applied to non-Western, noncapitalist societies, we must attempt to understand how structural formations work when economic forces are not dominant. How do such formations reproduce themselves, and what internal forces and contradictions are capable of generating structural change? How do the dynamics of capitalism interact with the existing mode(s) of production after contact?

In working out his theory on modes of production, Marx continued to think about noncapitalist societies and what made them different in terms of social organization and human relationships. But Marx's knowledge and understanding of "primitive" societies was limited by existing knowledge and European perceptions of non-Western societies in the nineteenth century. Not until the 1960s did a group of French anthropologists, influenced by Althusser, begin to analyze primitive societies in terms of structure and modes of production.[10] Anthropologists such as Claude Meillassoux, Maurice Godelier, Emmanuel Terray, and Pierre-Phillippe Rey integrated abstract structural concepts with empirical studies of African lineage societies. Marxist structural anthropology focused on issues that included relations between economic production and kinship; the dominance of ideology in noncapitalist social formations; exploitation, domination, and existence or nonexistence of class relations in noncapitalist societies; the articulation of different modes of production as societies change; and transformations of social and political relations when noncapitalist societies are penetrated by the forces of Western imperialism.[11]

In contrast to capitalist societies, where economic factors are dominant, in noncapitalist societies the ideological level of the social structure is dominant. Religion articulates relations between the human, the natural, and the supernatural; and between human categories of male and female, ruler and ruled, and appropriator and producer. Religion inscribes virtually all social practices and interprets every aspect of reality. There are no purely economic institutions in these societies because political and ideological forces dominate economic practices with kinship or hierarchy determining the place of individuals in production, their rights to land usage and goods, and their obligations in terms of work and gifts.

Religion, which prescribes the "lived relations" of the social structure, is active at the level of daily life (farming, fishing, eating, mating, sex, etc.), as well as in highly formalized, socially charged rituals that sanctify power and domination. In less complex societies, such as hunting and gathering communities, religion is omnipresent, but little organized institutionally. In societies such as Hawai'i and the Inca of Peru, however, complex religious organizations and practices sanctified social relationships, maintained the hierarchical divisions between sacred rulers and the less-sacred ruled, and ideologically resolved structural contradictions.[12]

Language and Power: Poststructuralist Perspectives

In the past decade or so, literary and cultural studies scholars have reengaged the Marxist problematic of the relations between the material world and human consciousness. These new theoretical efforts merged Marxist notions of ideology as representational practices with poststructuralist conceptualizations of knowledge, language, and power.[13] The social institutions, practices, and relationships most deeply inscribed by ideology are those that a society regards as natural or nothing more than common sense— the taken-for-granted that resides in language and the practices of language. Therefore, understanding the practices of language and discourse is of central importance in understanding the shifting relationships of power that began in Hawai'i with Western contact. As Hawaiians moved from orality to literacy, and as the Hawaiian language was supplanted by English as the medium of discourse, processes even more fundamentally important than the institution of capitalism were set in motion.

The theoretical problematization of language and society came to the fore in the twentieth century with Saussurean structuralism and Foucaultian-inspired poststructuralism. Both Ferdinand de Saussure and Michel Foucault placed language at the center of the social construction, perception, and knowledge of reality. But they differed profoundly in their stance toward history and their conceptualizations of linguistic practice as a locus of power. Saussure reacted against the historical orientation of nineteenth-century philology, taking instead a synchronic, structuralist orientation toward language. He posited that language is structured in difference and identity, that meaning is produced from the multidimensional, shifting relationships among signs: "All of which simply means that in language there are only differences."[14] Words are social conceptualizations of reality that are wholly arbitrary. Words are part of a linguistic structure that overlays the material world, constructing the way a community experiences the world. Language and social practices are interdependent, but not in an isomorphic, one-to-one relationship. Although a language is constantly changing in terms of the relationships among signs in the system, a number of forces ensure its continuity. The most important are institutionalized and communal social forces linked with time—education, religion, family relations, media— all the ways by which distinct communities pass their language from generation to generation. In all parts of the world, Western imperialism and colonialism disrupted communal social forces that had maintained linguistic continuity over centuries.

Although Saussure recognized external forces of change in a language (e.g., the intermingling of different people's languages, such as occurred prior to the formation of modern nation-states in Europe), his conceptualization of language change was basically an apolitical, evolutionary one.[15] He makes only brief reference to "discontinuities" of languages, placing such phenomena in a historical context where one of several coexisting languages gradually emerges as the "literary" language.

> By literary language I mean not only the language of literature but also, in a more general sense, any kind of cultivated language, official or otherwise, that *serves* the whole community. . . . But as communications improve with a growing civilization, one of the existing dialects *is chosen by a tacit convention of some sort* to be the vehicle of everything that affects the nation as a whole.[16]

Saussure's words are conspicuous for their apolitical view of language as a site of social struggle. In contrast, Nietzsche's (and later Foucault's) conceptualization of "the will to power" inscribed in language speaks more cogently to the experience of Hawai'i, where language, conflict, and power were inseparable. Language is not a neutral medium, but a hidden subjective power that shapes experience, defines reality, and says what is good, true, and beautiful. Practices of language construct our world by ordering and constraining our perceptions of it.[17] When Hawaiian was replaced by English as the dominant language of trade, politics, and instruction, power shifted into the hands of those whose assumptions of reality and discursive practices were shaped by English.

A structural analysis also looks at how ideologies shape symbolic practices. Chant and *hula* and later forms of Hawaiian music have been important expressive forms throughout Hawai'i's history. By looking at their transformations over time, particularly during that critical conjuncture of the nineteenth century when Western structures and practices took center stage in Hawai'i, we can understand the cultural and social implications of political and economic changes.[18] Chant, *hula,* and contemporary music are symbolizing practices that were (and are) shaped by successive structural formations in the islands. Jacques Attali has theorized the historical relationships between music and society.[19] These relationships are complex, shaped by the past, by dominant economic, political, and ideological relations and practices of the present, as well as technologies of music production. All these forces affect and are affected by the unique ways that music is produced, distributed, and consumed. In each transition period in the history of a society the old syntax of music is subverted by new syntax, old music forms are challenged by new forms, leading to new codes of music production and meaning:

> Every code of music is rooted in the ideologies and technologies of its age, and at the same time produces them. . . . The simultaneity of multiple codes, the variable overlapping between periods, styles, and forms, prohibits any attempt at a

genealogy of music. . . . What must be constructed, then, is more like a map, a structure of interferences and dependencies between society and its music.[20]

As an inscription of ideology, music legitimizes structures of power in several ways: by silencing history, by resolving social contradictions through projecting social harmony and order, and by silencing other musics.[21]

In this history I am looking at Hawaiian music not merely as ideological practices, but as discursive objects within successive discursive regimes. Chant, *hula*, and newer forms of Hawaiian music have been socially constituted and reconstituted into different objects and practices by different groups of people. The ideologies that have shaped the production of Hawaiian music over the past three centuries have been varied and conflicting. Music offers us, therefore, a way of understanding the larger social transformations that have taken place in Hawai'i.

Chapter Three

Hawai'i before Contact with the West

O ke au i kahuli wela ka honua
O ke au i kahuli lole ka lani
O ke au i kuka'iaka ka la
E ho'omalamalama i ka malama
O ke au o Makali'i ka po
O ka walewale ho'okumu honua ia
O ke kumu o ka lipo, i lipo ai
O ke kumu o ka Po, i po ai
O ka lipolipo, o ka lipolipo
O ka lipo o ka la, o ka lipo o ka po
    Po wale ho—'i
Hanau ka po
Hanau Kumulipo i ka po, he kane
Hanau Po'ele i ka po, he wahine

At the time when the earth became hot
At the time when the heavens turned about
At the time when the sun was darkened
To cause the moon to shine
The time of the rise of the Pleiades
The slime, this was the source of the earth
The source of the darkness that made darkness
The source of the night that made night
The intense darkness, the deep darkness
Darkness of the sun, darkness of the night
    Nothing but night.
The night gave birth
Born was Kumulipo in the night, a male
Born was Po'ele in the night, a female

Martha W. Beckwith, trans. and ed.,
The Kumulipo

I want to begin my structural analysis of Hawai'i before Western contact for two reasons. The first is to be able to compare the islands before Cook's arrival with what happened afterward so that the structural implications of capitalism can be better understood. The second is that I wish to avoid the dominant ethnocentric view of Pacific societies before Western contact as simple, primitive, and static, waiting, as it were, for the action to begin.

Hawai'i's history of structural transformations is as dynamic, contradictory, and conflictual as any the West can offer. With the problematization of the liberal progressive view of the islands—that Hawai'i can retain its beauty and charm and at the same time become the center of Pacific tourism and development—has emerged a countertendency to romanticize the islands before Western contact as a model of natural harmony. To so idealize the islands denies the complex society that Hawai'i was—a society of intellectual and technological achievements, a society that politically, religiously, and economically was neither primitive nor simple.

In this chapter I focus on three aspects of Hawai'i prior to contact with the West: the articulation of the ideological, political, and economic levels within the Hawaiian hierarchical mode of production;[1] the ideological reproduction of the social structure; and the contradictions that existed within that dominant mode and between that mode and an earlier, more communal mode of production.

Thinking about Hawai'i in terms of Marxist structural concepts requires a certain amount of imaginative play. It also requires a willingness to entertain the possibility that certain assumptions about social relationships derived from Western experience might be relevant to Hawaiian history. It certainly involves considerable essentializing, of looking through the lens of structural theories at broad outlines of Hawaiian social structures over time. There is no doubt that any history does violence to the richness of Hawai'i's past experience, to the differences between islands, and to manifestations of Hawaiian thought and experience over centuries of time. Nonetheless, with these caveats in mind, I believe that a structuralist interpretation offers significant insight into the past as well as the present conditions of these islands.

The Hawaiian Social Structure

In the century or so before Cook's arrival, Hawai'i was a tightly articulated social structure. In Althusserian terms, the ideological level was the "structure in dominance." Religion governed the political and economic elements of the social totality, with all aspects of human relationships and practices religiously constituted and infused with sacred meaning.[2] Religion determined the status of groups and individuals, and religion was the basis for the allocation, appropriation, and distribution of land and goods. In short, religion constituted the "lived relations" of Hawaiians. Hawai'i was a highly stratified social structure, with power concentrated in the ruling *ali'i*. The supreme embodiments of both sacred and secular power (there was no significant distinction between the two) were the highest ruling chiefs, variously referred to as the *ali'i nui* (the high chief), the *mō'ī* (king), or *ali'i'aimoku* (paramount chief of a territory, usually an island).

The Ideological: Kapu *and* Mana

The religious, ideological principles of *mana* and subsidiary notions of *kapu* and *noa* determined and constrained all social relations and informed the material practices of Hawai'i. *Mana,* a complex, Polynesianwide concept, has been conceptualized by anthropologists as process, performance, power, abstract force, and effect, or as all these things. *Mana* was the positive manifestation of spirituality and power—power that emanated from the gods and was channeled through the *ali'i,* power that was embedded in the forces of nature (weather, volcanoes, the fertility of crops), in human knowledge and skills, in procreation and fertility, in cycles of birth and death; and power that was evident in the social well-being of the community. *Mana,* the life force that came from the gods, infused all of nature—plants and animals, sky and water, places and people—but the greatest concentration of *mana* was in the highest *ali'i,* the most divine and most powerful chiefs, who received it through their sacred genealogical links to the gods.[3]

The associated practices and notions of *kapu* and *noa* were equally complex and ambiguous. Associated with sacredness, power, and control, *kapu* and *noa* maintained the hierarchical relations that characterized the Hawaiian social system.[4] *Kapu* determined what was sacred and forbidden; *noa,* what was not divine and, therefore, free of *kapu.* Persons or things were *kapu* (or *noa*) because they were tied (or not tied) to the sacred powers of the gods and the transmission of that power through god/human/ material relationships. *Kapu* included the sacred prohibitions and privileges that determined how an individual or groups of individuals related to the gods, to each other, and to the material resources of the islands (e.g., who could eat what, wear what, go where, and who could appropriate and use various natural and societal resources). *Ali'i* and their powers were divine and therefore maintained and protected by *kapu.* The genealogy, genitals, clothing, actions, even the spit, of the highest *ali'i* were sacred and therefore protected by *kapu.*

Within the *maka'āinana, kapu* governed relations between men and women and regulated the use of resources. Men, associated with light, air, rain, and Wākea—the Sky Father—were included within the sacred aspects of life; women, associated with the earth, darkness, and Papa—the Earth Mother—were prohibited from eating certain foods, entering certain places, and participating in certain activities, generally inscribed within the *kapu* of defilement.[5] Sexuality and relations of gender were ambiguous, however: women's procreative powers were not only sources of pollution but also sources of *mana.*[6]

In the finely graded hierarchical system of Hawai'i, *kapu* inscribed a complex and elaborate system of superior and inferior that "marked" and indexed status separations within the ranks of the *ali'i*, as well as between *ali'i* and *maka'āinana*, men and women, and between all of the above and the *kauwā* (outcasts or slaves), those outside the social perimeters of Hawaiian society.[7] Not only did *kapu* inscribe social relationships; *kapu* was part of all productive practices, such as farming, fishing, canoe building, house construction, and the making of tools and weapons. From the beginning of a project to its completion, *kapu* prescribed how it was to be done, the materials to be used, who could work on it, and the rituals that were to be observed along the way.[8] In short, *mana* and *kapu* were ideological practices that legitimated political authority, allocated the forces of production, and ordered all social relations, including the relations of production.

If *kapu* maintained social and personal order through a combination of discipline and coercion, *mana* was what the *ali'i* offered in return for the obedience and tribute of the *maka'āinana*. The wealth and military success of a *mō'ī* and the fertility of his land were evidence of the strength of his *mana*; defeat or conditions of drought were manifestations of its weakness.[9] Therefore, while *mana*, like *kapu*, was inherited by *ali'i* through their kinship with the gods, *ali'i* at the highest levels of power (or those aiming at that level) were constantly engaged in securing, demonstrating and increasing their *mana*—their power.[10]

Traced back to divine transmission, the potency defined by *mana* is necessarily unstable and mobile. Simply put, *mana* is not simply possessed; it is appropriated, and at time even wrested from its divine sources. . . . Implicitly, then, precontact Polynesian religion was an economy of *mana* in which generative powers were appropriated, channeled, transformed, and bound. Because such potency was constructive only when properly channeled, Polynesians characteristically lived in a very dangerous world. . . . The set of beliefs and practices in Polynesia associated with the transformation in *mana* are virtually coextensive with Polynesian religion and much of what we call politics as well.[11]

The Political: Ali'i *and the Priesthood*

Political and religious power were virtually one and the same in Hawai'i.[12] Power was institutionalized in the elaborated hierarchical system of Hawai'i, legitimized by *ali'i* genealogy, protected by *kapu*, and demonstrated in and through material manifestations of *mana*. Power resided in the position of the *mō'ī*, which only ranking *ali'i* were entitled to hold or aspire to, in a pyramidal governmental system that extended in a chain of command from the *mō'ī* through successively lower levels of chiefs managing successively smaller sections of the polity. The governing of a *mō'ī's* domain had become extremely complex by the eighteenth century. Power was concentrated in the hands of a few high chiefs, each of whom controlled all or a major part of an island.[13] Administering a territory of that size required considerable organization and staff, including administrative officers, military leaders, religious specialists, and stewards to maintain the chief's lands, storehouses, and household goods.[14]

Buttressing this political structure were institutionalized priesthoods. The two most important priesthoods were those of Kū, the god associated with war, and Lono, the god associated with peace and fertility. Both the Kū and Lono priesthoods had their own separate systems of *heiau* (temples) and their own religious rites. By the eighteenth century they were heavily ritualized, with *kāhuna pule* (priests who were specialists in praying) at the top ranks, paralleling the hierarchical structure of the *ali'i*. The Kū priesthood was the highest ranking, and its rituals were conducted within *luakini heiau* (Kū temples) that were accessible only to the *mō'ī*, his top *ali'i*, and the Kū priesthood. But not all religious practice was inscribed within the purview of the major gods and their priesthoods. There were family gods and many other gods, worshipped by *ali'i* and by the *maka'āinana*, that were outside the confines of institutionalized religious structures.[15]

The Economic Level: Tribute and Land

Hawai'i's hierarchical political structure and its system of economic appropriation have been characterized as "feudal" or "feudal-like," or described in feudalistic terms, that is, having an "aristocracy," "nobility," and "serfs."[16] Feudalism implies a different system of land tenure, however, and a different kind of relationship between rulers and ruled than existed in Hawai'i. Under European feudalism, the lord's power came from his land, which was valued because it enabled him to reward his professional warriors for their bravery and loyalty. Maintaining the allegiance of fiefs or knights was vital in a society where social order was extremely tenuous. As feudal relationships evolved in Europe, land became the inherited property of a class of nobles, and feudal laws were oriented to protecting property rights, thereby sustaining the rights of feudal lords to extract a surplus from land that belonged to them and the serfs who were bound to the land.[17]

The Hawaiian hierarchical mode of production was similar to European feudalism in its hierarchical ordering of power and its system of first-fruits tribute—the institutionalized appropriation of goods by the ruling *ali'i*, which Western observers generally referred to as "taxation." But, in Hawai'i, land was allocated and reallocated by each new *mō'ī*, and *maka'āinana* were not legally bound to it, as serfs were in feudal Europe.[18] Furthermore, the complex reciprocal relationships linking land, gods, *ali'i*, and *maka'āinana* were spiritually different from those of medieval Christian Europe.[19]

Just as religion determined political relations, so it also articulated economic production. Forces and relations of production were religiously inscribed and embedded in the political system of chieftainship. Status-seeking chiefs needed a surplus of food and goods for ritual obligations, for maintaining their chiefly apparatus, for redistribution to their supporting *ali'i*, for status (evidence of *kapu* and *mana*), and for warfare. Given the structure of Hawaiian society and the dynamics involved in securing and maintaining power, a constant or increasing level of surplus was needed to reproduce the hierarchical social structure. It was the hierarchical social system, synonymous with the relations of production (the relationship between a nonfood-producing class and the productive *maka'āinana*), that organized production and linked the *maka'āinana* to the land, to the chiefs, and to the gods in a complex social matrix.[20] Control over land, and the resources generated from land, constituted the ultimate outward measure of the status and power of a *mō'ī*. Land was allocated to *ali'i* for their use and management only as long as it pleased the *mō'ī*. Through power over land, the *mō'ī* controlled the productive relations and resources of his territory. If he was defeated, his land passed into the hands of the conquering chief for reapportionment among his supporting *ali'i*.[21]

Ahupua'a were the basic operating land divisions, and the natural boundaries of community life. They were generally pie-shaped wedges of land that stretched from the shore to the uplands, offering those who lived there access to a range of needed resources for their own sustenance and for the surpluses that must be provided for chiefly consumption. The *ali'i* given responsibility for managing an *ahupua'a*, called *konohiki*, supervised farming and irrigation, collected "taxes," organized corvée labor (for construction of temples, war canoes, and large-scale irrigation and aquaculture systems), conscripted men and weapons for military activities, and provided for the needs of the *mō'ī's* large retinue. David Malo, a nineteenth-century, missionary-educated Hawaiian scholar, makes it clear that there were penalties if goods were not forthcoming from the *maka'āinana* and that these penalties were "shared" through successive layers of managing *ali'i*.

The major period for the appropriation of tribute came in the fall, during the *makahiki*. A time of religious observances honoring Lono, the god of agricultural productivity and fertility, the *makahiki* was marked by the offering of the yearly tribute; by celebrations of feasting, games, and sports; and by the closing of the *heiau* of Kū, the god of war. Malo describes the collection of tribute during the *makahiki* as follows:

> In the succeeding days the Makahiki taxes were gotten ready against the coming of the tax collectors. . . . It was the duty of the konohiki to collect in the first place all the property which was levied from the loa for the king; each konohiki also brought tribute for his own landlord, which was called waiwai maloko. . . . On . . . (the twentieth day), the levying of taxes was completed, and the property that had been collected was displayed before the gods (hoomoe ia): and on the following day (olekukahi), the king distributed it among the chiefs and the companies of soldiery throughout the land. . . . No share of this property . . . was given to the people.[22]

In return for their labor and tribute, *maka'āinana* had usage rights to cultivate the *ahupua'a* where they lived. Although they had no absolute right to the land, usage rights were rarely disrupted even with a wholesale shift of power at the top. The right of an *'ohana* (an extended family) to live in and use a portion of an *ahupua'a* usually passed from generation to generation as long as labor and tributary demands were met.[23] In addition to economic security, *maka'āinana* received equally important religious and psychological benefits. "While little probably filtered down to the *maka'āinana*, their benefit, however symbolic, was nonetheless real. Their land had been revitalized by the God in whose honor they had given tribute. The land could now feed them as it had been touched by the *Akua*, who was Lono and who, in another mystical sense, was the *Mō'ī*."[24]

Ideological Reproduction

Power in Hawai'i, although structured into a particular constellation of social relationships, was far from static; power was continuously contested and challenged among *ali'i*. But, these "natural" processes of political conflict did not affect structured relations of power—the actors changed, but the plot remained essentially the same. Once ensconced into the position of ruling authority over an existing territorial domain, a *mōʻī* could increase his power only by enlarging or enhancing his chiefdom through territorial aggrandizement. This could be accomplished through war, through "marriage," or through political affiliations with other *mōʻī*. Status was also affirmed and enhanced by the accumulation of material manifestations of wealth, such as larger surpluses of crops for political redistribution, war canoes, feather capes, and other political insignia and symbols of rank; as well as by gestures of wealth or benevolence, such as increased subsidization of the priesthoods, craftsmen, and artists, and by bigger celebration feasts.[25]

The institutions and practices of religion reproduced the hierarchical structure of Hawaiian society. Although there were numerous gods, including personal family gods of *aliʻi* and *makaʻāinana*, the gods of living things and physical features of the land, and gods of the various occupational orders ("the forty thousand gods, the four hundred thousand gods, the four thousand gods"), four major god categories encompassed, through their particularized forms, almost every aspect of reality: Kū, Lono, Kāne, and Kanaloa.[26] There were hierarchical relationships within the ranks of the gods that corresponded to social status. Therefore, an individual could make temple sacrifices only to those gods that matched his hierarchical position in society.

Because sacrificial rituals were integral to major events, as well as to recurring cyclical rites of day-to-day life (i.e., rituals for stages of the life cycle; rituals for planting, eating, and work; rituals for expiation and purification; first-fruits sacrificial rituals; and so on), there was constant reaffirmation of the hierarchical relationships within the social structure.[27] For instance, during the *makahiki*, the *mōʻī* was the chief actor, the focus (in his association with the god Lono) of the people's attention and devotion. The elaborated *makahiki* system validated the land rights of the *mōʻī* and his supporting *aliʻi*—the rituals of tribute constituting the redistribution of goods from *maka'āinana* to chiefs as spiritual acts, as symbolic and material reaffirmations of the *mō'ī* as "the life of the land and of the people."[28] The *mana* of the *mō'ī*, coming from the gods, was thus ritually and publicly reaffirmed by the people as the spiritual source of the fertility of the land and their prosperity. This reciprocity between leaders and those led was positively affirmed in the ideology of *aloha*, a spiritual bond between ruling *ali'i* and *maka'āinana*.

There were two main kinds of *kāhuna*. The more important were the *heiau kāhuna*, particularly *kāhuna pule*, who officiated in the *heiau* alongside the *mō'ī*. They were the masters of the word, who actualized meaning in speech. The power of the temple priests lay in their control of religious and historical knowledge and ritual, in their role in enforcing *kapu*, and in their command of the genealogies and oral histories—not only because they held them in their prodigious memories but also because they were skilled in creating and refashioning genealogies to legitimate a *mō'ī's* claim to power or to remove, if needed, any taint of defilement. According to Malo, genealogists were called the "wash-basins of the *ali'i* in which to cleanse them"[29] In Foucaultian terms, the priesthood constituted a "society of discourse."[30]

The second major category of priests were specialists in the ritualized practices of daily life—priests associated with medicine and productive activities such as canoe building, fishing, and farming. Their involvement with the practices of everyday life made them as integral to the ideological reproduction of the social structure as the ritual priests who officiated in the temples. Both categories of priests were integral to what Althusser would call the "ideological apparatus" of Hawaiian society.[31]

Hierarchical relations were legitimated in *ali'i* genealogies.[32] Genealogies determined privileges of *kapu* for the *ali'i* and were therefore central to structured relations of power. Although in practice genealogical rank often followed wealth and power, rather than the other way round, genealogy did set parameters for who could contend for power, limiting struggles over power to *ali'i* who were able by birth to fashion a genealogy befitting their rank or claimed rank.[33] Genealogy was, therefore, taken very seriously. Consequently, mating—inserting oneself and one's children as high into the sacred ranks as possible—was extremely important. Although genealogy was prescriptive and limiting, it was also ambiguous, a site and practice of argument and challenge. The ambiguity of genealogy arose primarily from the practice among *ali'i* of having more than one chiefly "wife," thereby fathering multiple first-born sons of high rank. This produced claimants of equal or near-equal genealogies to challenge allocations of power. A *mō'ī*, therefore had continuously to protect his power from other amibitious *ali'i*, not only from rival families, but from within his own. Usurpation was structured into the social system and was therefore a recurring phenomenon. The result was cyclical disruptions of power through war.[34]

Once an *ali'i* "proved" his genealogical claim, *kapu* protected it and reproduced it. The most godlike of the *ali'i* maintained their own level of sacredness through the privileges of *kapu* they commanded, and that of their future offspring by mating with someone of identical genealogical standing—by definition, a sister. The children from such a mating were protected by the most stringent of all the sacred *kapu*, the *kapu ā moe*, which required all persons, including other *ali'i*, to prostrate themselves or suffer death. According to Malo, such an *ali'i* would go out only at night because if he went during "open day (when people were about their usual avocations), every one had to fall to the ground in an attitude of worship" to keep his shadow from falling on the chief—the penalty would be death. A slightly less sacred mating was between a *mō'ī* and his half-sister or niece; their offspring would be accorded the sitting *kapu*, the *kapu ā noho*.[35] And so on down the genealogical ladder—*ali'i* of lesser genealogical ranks entitled to lesser signs of deference. According to Malo, "the great chiefs were entirely exclusive, being hedged about with many tabus, and a large number of people were slain for breaking, or infringing upon, these tabus. The tabus that hedged about an alii were exceedingly strict and severe."[36]

The dynamic nature of the Hawaiian status system and the ambiguity inherent in it required continuing readjustments between formal principles and shifting conditions, between complex ideological practices of status ascription and the reality of accommodating achievement, between sacred and secular interests, between the formal and the pragmatic. "The values of status are . . . in part given, traditional, axiomatic, and thus objective; and in part created anew in each situation and so remeasured and reevaluated, and thus ultimately subjective. . . . Ambiguity is not to be taken as a "failing" in the system, but rather as an integral aspect of its inherent tensions."[37]

Chant and *Hula*: At the Ideological Center

There were numerous types of chants in Hawaiian society. Some were created by *maka'āinana*, others by *ali'i* and priests. Many were performed publicly, including chants praising the reigning *mō'ī*, game chants, love chants, lamentation chants, and chants improvised for special or informal occasions; others were performed only within the walls of *heiau* for the most powerful *ali'i* and priests. But all chants, even those performed for fun and entertainment, had religious meanings, hence political connotations.[38]

As ideological practice, chant and *hula* were forms of social representation that maintained relationships of power and difference by expressing and legitimating the authority of the religious–political system.[39] The most religiously powerful chants were those that celebrated the high chiefs and demonstrated their descendance from the gods and sacred *ali'i* of the past. These chants were infused with *mana* and protected by *kapu*. There were cosmological and genealogical chants that recounted the creation of the world and the familial relationships of contemporary *ali'i* to *ali'i* of the past. *Mele inoa* (name chants) were more or less sacred depending on the rank of the *ali'i* being praised and the occasion. The most sacred chants could be chanted only by *kāhuna* at ceremonies and in temple areas restricted to *ali'i* and priests.[40]

A sociology of the culture of eighteenth-century Hawai'i would show that the social contexts of chant creation and performance varied by social status. At the top of the social hierarchy were large *hālau* (schools) associated with major *heiau*, at the lower levels of the *ali'i* were less formal and smaller *hālau* and *heiau*, and at the *maka'āinana* level were family groups and troops of dancers that would move around an island performing for in-kind, informal contributions.[41] The most heavily ritualized chants and *hula* were institutionalized within overlapping power structures of the *ali'i* and the priesthoods. A *mō'ī* had within his immediate circle of top officials and specialists highly trained individuals called *haku mele* (composers), usually *kāhuna* specifically charged with composing and performing chants and maintaining the chief's genealogy. Also supported by high chiefs were *hālau* under the direction of *kumu hula* (teachers of *hula*) in which selected individuals (*ali'i* and *maka'āinana*) were trained in the ritual and art of chant and *hula*. It was the responsibility of the *hālau* members—the priests, the *kumu hula*, the chanters, the dancers—to compose, maintain, and perform the chants of the *ali'i*, particularly chants about their genealogical and chiefly qualities that legitimized power. For instance, Malo reports that preceding the birth of a new *ali'i*, the *haku mele* would compose a *mele inoa* for the new chief-to-be. The *mele* would be committed to memory, a *hula* choreographed to accompany it, the *hula* then taught to those who would perform it until the child was born.[42]

The rules and conventions that organized the practice of religious ritual prescribed and maintained the formalism of chant and *hula*. To be a member of a *hālau* required special education and arduous training. It was "a religious matter to be guarded against profanation by the observance of tabus and the performance of priestly rites."[43] In short, the production of chant and *hula* was institutionalized at the center of the most important of the ideological apparatus, an apparatus that fused divine kingship and the supporting priesthood. Captain George Vancouver's description of a *hula* he observed in 1794 at a ceremony to honor the coming birth of an *ali'i* child shows the care and precision accorded to such ceremonies:

> The entertainment consisted of three parts, and was per-
> formed by three different parties consisting of about two
> hundred women in each, who ranged themselves in five or six
> rows, not standing up, not kneeling, but rather sitting upon
> their haunches. . . . The whole of this numerous group was in
> perfect unison of voice and action, that it were impossible,
> even to the bend of a finger, to have discerned the least varia-
> tion. Their voices were melodious, and their actions were as
> innumerable as, by me, they are undescribable; they exhibited
> great ease and much elegance, and the whole was executed
> with a degree of correctness not easily to be imagined.[44]

The narrative content and forms of chant expressed the dominant representation of human and sacred relationships. Chant
gave coherence and continuity to the Hawaiian social structure,
containing and interpreting events and social relations in a way
that generalized, extended, and crystalized the dominant view of
an idealized past, present, and future. By the eighteenth century,
chant and *hula* constituted what Northrup Frye calls "myths of
concern": "They are the stories that tell a society what is important for it to know, whether about its gods, its history, its laws, or
its class structure. . . . They thus become "sacred" as distinct from
"profane" stories, and form part of what the Biblical tradition calls
revelation."[45]

Chants were ideological representations that framed history
and relationships of domination in ways that resolved some contradictions and masked others. Chants textualized and maintained traditional authority, not because they explained reality,
but because they hid it. The power of ritualized forms of representation lies in their ability to naturalize a situation of domination,

to idealize relationships that bind one group to another.[46] Most accounts of Hawai'i's past obscure the dynamics of ideological practice, how the content of chants were manipulated to serve political interests, what Sahlins call "mytho-praxis," or Foucault, "discourses of power."[47] The *Kumulipo,* for instance, the great Hawaiian creation chant, is a composite work that was revised and reworked many times to incorporate new genealogies to older genealogies and cosmological accounts of the universe. On one known occasion in the eighteenth century it was chanted to celebrate the new *ali'i* child, Lonoikamakahiki; when it was first written down in the nineteenth century it was again a politically symbolic act, linking the elected king, Kalākaua, to an ancestral line that the *Kumulipo* traced back through generations of sacred *ali'i* to the gods.[48] Although chants were consciously manipulated and used to legitimize the political claims of particular *ali'i,* the real ideological power of chants lay not so much in their words but in their codes, conventions, and ideologemes. Chants were symbolic enactments that allocated identities, integrating *mō'ī, ali'i* priests, and *maka'āinana* into shared imaginary representations of reality. As ideological acts, they resolved social contradictions, defining Hawaiian society as much by what they excluded as by what they included.

Structure and Change before Contact

In Chapter Two, I discussed the Marxist concept of mode of production and the coexistence of more than one mode of production in any given society at any given time. Such a situation produces contradictions within a society that may or may not rupture the social structure, depending on the nature of the contradictions, the presence of outside forces, and the ability of ideological forces and practices to resolve and mask contradictions.

There is evidence of two coexisting modes of production in Hawai'i at the close of the eighteenth century: a communal mode of production surviving from earlier historical periods that was based on reciprocity among communal members and was still operative among the extended territorially based families of the *maka'āinana*; and the hierarchical mode of production that was the dominant mode in determining the overall relations of production in eighteenth-century Hawai'i. Within each, production, distribution, and redistribution of resources and political power operated under two fundamentally different principles: the communal mode articulated by an ideology of reciprocity and relative equality; and the other, the dominant hierarchical mode, operating under principles of enforced tribute and surplus appropriation legitimized by principles of divine kingship. Production and circulation of goods within the former mode was use determined, while in the latter production and consumption were measures of status and affirmations of social hierarchy. The first was a domestic, household economy; the other, an honorific economy.[49] By the late eighteenth century, the hierarchical relations of the dominant mode of production had developed to the point where there was the equivalent of a class-divided society.[50]

The Development of Coexisting Modes of Production

That there were two synchronically existing modes of production during the eighteenth century raises questions about their historical roots and their articulation with each other. Oral traditions suggest that a second migration of Polynesians introduced significant political and religious changes. Another view, while accepting a second migratory period, looks more to internal developments to explain the development of a hierarchical social structure. It is safe to say that the transformation of the social structure resulted from a combination of forces arising from internal and externally introduced forces.

The migratory theory elaborates a theme in Hawaiian oral tradition: settlement of the islands by two migrations. The initial settlers came from the Marquesas Islands; the second migration from the Society Islands (including Tahiti). The latter had among them *ali'i* and priests, including the historically prominent Kū priest Pā'ao. This second wave of immigrants supposedly introduced a new chiefly line and a more extreme form of social hierarchy than before, a harsher system of *kapu*, new *heiau* forms such as the *luakini*-type *heiau* of the Kū priesthood, and elaborate religious rituals from which the *maka'āinana* were excluded, including rituals of human sacrifice associated with the war god Kū.[51] For instance, Malo and Kamakau imply that *kapu* associated with the practice of daily acitivities—the division of labor within the family, male and female eating practices, and activities concerned with canoe building, fishing, planting, and harvesting— were older than the extremely harsh *kapu* regulating hierarchical social relations between and among *ali'i* and *maka'āinana*.[52]

The archaeologist Patrick Kirch does not dispute the occurrence of later migrations, but he rejects the social significance that has been attached to the second period of migration. He explains social change in Hawai'i as primarily the result of internal processes that occurred locally in isolation from other Polynesian influences, such as increased competition among chiefs for land and resources that generated ranking kinds of *kapu* and more frequent warfare, the latter resulting in increased power of the Kū priesthood within the social structure. Drawing on his own research and that of other archaeologists,[53] Kirch outlines four phases of social development. The first was the initial settlement period, which lasted from roughly A.D. 300–600. The first settlements were on the most arable areas of the islands' coasts, with the people sustained primarily by an "occupying" economy (use of "found" resources with simple cultivation) and united within corporate descent groups. Although the first settlers brought with them Polynesianwide concepts of chiefly hierarchy, first-fruits tribute, and chiefly intercession with the gods, the early chiefs were senior members of a descent group and not a separate class, as later developed.

During the second phase (from approximately 600 to 1100), people continued to adapt their agricultural and marine production techniques to meet the Hawaiian environment, forming in the process a unique cultural variation of the basic ancestral Polynesian system. The gap between chiefs and commoners widened, but still it was not distinct enough for the two groups to be considered separate classes. The third phase was the expansion period from 1100 to 1650. This period was marked by intensified agricultural production with the construction of irrigation and dryfield systems, as well as the intensification of aquaculture in the form of coastal fishponds—the beginning of a transformative economy taking shape alongside the productive practices of the earlier period. A large population increase occurred during this time, which was a major factor in the technological, social, and political changes that took place. There was increasing economic specialization and extensive use of corvée labor for large-scale public works projects such as irrigation systems, fish-pond building, and *heiau* construction. New productive forces transformed conditions of production, relations of production, and forms of political authority. These more complex divisions of labor and unequal distribution of goods and resources required forms of centralized management and control, resulting in social structures that were significantly different from those based on more traditional kinship relations and communal production.[54]

As these new relations of production developed, local communities' control over resource development and distribution was diminished, increasingly so as the society became more stratified and the hierarchical mode of production became the dominant mode. In effect, a separate productive organization developed, at first alongside the existing communal practices, but eventually dominating them. The ideological incorporation of communal practices into the new relations of production was facilitated by already existing notions of hierarchy and first-fruits tribute. But instead of relations of production embedded in extended family groups, social divisions between *ali'i* and *maka'āinana* were increasingly differentiated. As land units became more or less fixed along lines of chiefly held territories that expanded and contracted and confirming the divisions of society, the exaltation of the nobles and the increase of their prerogatives, the separation and immunity of the priestly order, and the systematic setting down, if not actual debasement, of the commoners, the Makaainana.[57]

The final phase lasted from 1650 to Kamehameha's conquest of O'ahu in 1795. This was a time of further elaboration of developments initiated during the previous period: greater intensification of agriculture; further development of the chiefly status system with increasing ritualization and a harsher system of *kapu*; struggles for succession to chiefly power by junior members of *ali'i* families; more emphasis on marriages with high-ranking female *ali'i,* who became the primary transmitters of rank and *mana,* and who were therefore central to struggles over status and power; and the further rise of the Kū priesthood and the construction of large *luakini heiau* for rituals that included human sacrifice. It was a period marked by cycles of conquest, integration of districts, usurpation of power, collapse, and finally centralization of political control under Kamehameha I. It was also the time of initial intrusion by the West.

By the eighteenth century, large-scale political systems had developed. Agricultural intensification (for greater yields needed to support a large population and satisfy the demands of the chiefly status system) had resulted in the exploitation of marginal as well as arable lands. When Cook arrived, he found elaborate terracing, complex irrigation schemes, and labor-intensive farming practices. Kirch explains this level of development as the result of a complex combination of sociopolitical, demographic, and environmental factors.

It is insufficient, however, to explain agricultural intensification as a simple response to increased populations or even to chiefly competition. We must take into account the structure of Polynesian societies themselves, societies that were fundamentally hierarchical and pyramidal, in which chiefs actively stimulated production beyond the level of the individual household for the support of the greater public economy. . . . Surplus agricultural production was in the chiefs' interest, for such production financed their own efforts at hegemony through conquest, and at glorification of descent though the construction of monumental temples and other public works. . . . Irrigation, and other forms of agricultural (and aquacultural) intensification are thus seen as a form of capital investment, the concomitant increases in production used to support the competitive actions of the ruling chiefs.[58]

Hommon has argued that in the late 1700s Hawai'i was in fact a prestate political formation, the culmination of consolidating processes that had been going on over a period of approximately two hundred years prior to contact. He cites as evidence of Hawai'i's prestate formations the following: the disintegration of kinship-based land holdings, the formation of distinct economic and social classes, centralized control of governmental power, the replacement of simple redistributive economic relations between *ali'i* and *maka'āinana* by large-scale economic and social mobilization, and the maintenance of territories by force and a complex system of administrative control.

Domination and Conflict:
Structural Contradictions

The transformation between the communal mode of production and the hierarchical mode was not sudden (such as occurred during the capitalist transformation in the next century) but was one of gradual, discontinuous change similar in pace to the transformation of Europe from feudalism to capitalism. At the time of contact with the West, the two coexisting modes seemed to be in a state of *relative* accommodation, with contradictions between the two resolved or masked by the religious ideology that fused instances within the two modes, as well as the articulation between the modes. But there is evidence that social contradictions did exist. In a social system in which the ambiguous articulation of principles of succession generated rebellion, usurpations of power, and frequent territorial wars, political struggle was embedded in the principles of genealogy, of *ali'i* mating practices, and of land as the index of status. These structured contradictions *within* the dominant mode were evident in *ali'i* struggles over land and the power to exploit its resources and the continual processes of centralization and decentralization of political control.

The contradictions *between* coexisting modes are less clear in their effect. The occasional overthrow of abusive *ali'i* by *maka'āinana* points to strains resulting from excessive demands by the hierarchical system on the *maka'āinana*—the tendency for ruling chiefs "to eat the powers of the government too much."[59] Particularly during the eighteenth century, when warfare seems to have been virtually endemic, the dominant hierarchical mode generated demands for manpower (for armies and for the production of material implements of war such as weapons and canoes) and resources that must have interfered with the *maka'āinana* communal system of production and distribution.[60] Shifts in the political control of territories (the redividing of land and hence the imposition of new *konohiki* reporting to a new *mō'ī* as a result of victories and defeats among *ali'i* had to have had some impact on daily practices on production, resulting in tensions, at least intermittently, between the demands of the dominant hierarchical relations of production and the needs of communal relations of production at the *ahupua'a* level. Accounts in Malo of the *maka'āinana* occasionally overthrowing *ali'i* can be seen as evidence of these structural contradictions.[61]

In summary, when Cook arrived, Hawaiian society had undergone a transformation of structure from the ancient Polynesian communal system brought to Hawai'i by the first settlers to a highly stratified structure. This transformation adversely affected the status of the *maka'āinana* over time, concomitantly enhancing the power of ruling *ali'i*.

By the time of European contact, Hawaiian society had undergone two fundamental departures from Ancestral Polynesian Society, which highlight the degree of structural transformation. Both of these changes can be couched in negative terms from the viewpoint of the common people; they lost their genealogies, and they lost direct control of their land. The two, of course, descent and land, went hand-in-hand in Polynesia, and having lost one it is not surprising that they should have given up the other. More precisely, Hawaiian society had come to comprise a conical clan of chiefs superposed over a truncated class of commoners who worked the land and paid tribute to their lords.[62]

Based on the apparent absence of generalized class consciousness (a feeling of Us *against* Them), however, the contradictions that existed generated only sporadic conflict between *maka'āinana* and *ali'i*, nothing of a nature sufficient to threaten the hegemony of the dominant social structure at that historical conjuncture.

Domination involves both consent and violence.[63] In Hawai'i, consent was embedded in the ideological relations that normalized and naturalized the fundamental principles of social hierarchy: beliefs shared by all that *ali'i* were divinely endowed with *mana* and hence were legitimate rulers and that the *maka'āinana*'s natural role was to support the *ali'i* as the sacred and therefore political leaders of the people. This ideological construction of the rightness of existing social relations was deeply embedded in symbolic and material practices; it was truly hegemonic based on shared beliefs and popular consent.

Nevertheless, *ali'i* domination also rested on practices of violence and coercion. The system of *kapu* had become increasingly strict and violent as the hierarchical mode of production moved into the structural position of dominance. The severity of the *kapu* system and the extended social rituals that accompanied not only the major events in a *mō'ī*'s life but also his daily activities (his eating, his clothing, his going about among the people, even his spit and shadow) served to project, protect, and enforce the hierarchical status of the *ali'i* over the *maka'āinana* and, even more important, within the ranks of the *ali'i*—the primary site of social struggle. Maurice Bloch notes that the amount of ritual in a society is related to the amount of hierarchy and inequality in it: "Some inequality is often manifested as unadorned oppression, but, as Weber pointed out, it is then highly unstable, and only become stable when its origins are hidden and when it transforms itself into hierarchy: a legitimate order of inequality in an imaginary world which we call social structure."[64] The accepted, but also enforced, codes of power and social relations meant that the inequality and exploitation that existed were taken for granted as natural and sacred, and subordination was not perceived by the *maka'āinana* or lesser *ali'i* as demeaning. Class consciousness, in Marxist terms, did not exist.[65]

The absence of generalized struggles between *ali'i* and *maka'āinana* in effect "proved" the rightness of the existing social system. The system seemed to work, verifying in its very reproduction that the imaginary and the real coincided. Ralston characterizes the *maka'āinana* as "affluent subsistence farmers who were self-sufficient in terms of nearly all the essentials of life, albeit in a politically rather unstable world."[66] The consent of the *maka'āinana* was legitimized by the proven *mana* of the *mō'ī* in securing the blessings of the gods. Even the reported instances of *maka'āinana* rising up against particularly odious chiefs did not violate the fundamental relationship between ruling *ali'i* and *maka'āinana*, for in those cases *ali'i* were replaced by other *ali'i*, the structure reproduced in the act of rebellion and chiefly replacement, affirming the belief that it was only natural that *ali'i* ruled.

Because Hawaiian culture was more performative than prescriptive, cultural categories were readily manipulated for pur-

Chapter Four

Western Penetration and Structural Transformation

 How well do Western social, political, and cultural theories speak to the historical and contemporary experiences of a complex "peripheral" society such as that of Hawai'i? How well do they address the kinds of changes that resulted from the collision of societies of such unequal political, economic, and physical power? Marxist conceptualizations of modes of production and social transformations and poststructuralist theories of language, knowledge, and power are grounded in Western experience and Western metaphors of reality. Their application to the historical experiences of non-Western societies is therefore problematic.

One view is that all Western theories are so thoroughly ethnocentric that they are irrelevant or, worse, another violation of other histories and cultures by Western discourses of knowing. Another view, and one that I share, is that Marxist and poststructuralist concepts problematize dominant Western perceptions of social history, and therefore open the door for alternative accounts of Western imperialism and its continuing legacies. Even if we entertain the assumption that these theories are relevant to an understanding of Hawaiian history, we still must recognize fundamental differences in the historical transformation from feudalism to capitalism in Europe and the penetration of capitalism and Western culture into a society such as Hawai'i's. These differences may be thought of as both quantitative and qualitative in nature.

By quantitative differences, I am referring primarily to time (the rapidity with which capitalism dominated the islands) but also to space (the capitalist penetration of the total island chain). In Europe, the process of transformation from feudalism to capitalism took place over several centuries, in a process that was long and discontinuous; in Hawai'i, capitalism was imposed over a period of roughly fifty years and consolidated over the next half century or so. In Europe, many areas were slowly incorporated into the capitalist structure because of their distance from centers of trade and industry;[1] in Hawai'i, with its small land area, capitalist saturation was relatively rapid, particularly with the rise of the sugar industry after the middle of the nineteenth century.

In terms of qualitative differences between the European and Hawaiian experiences, a number of factors can be pointed to. Most of them come down to endogenous versus exogenous forces propelling capitalism. European capitalism was, comparatively speaking, "homegrown." Although capitalism did not spring up simultaneously throughout Europe, and therefore in some areas capitalism was more exogenous than in others, still capitalism came out of a more or less common feudal culture and history.[2] In contrast, capitalism was totally foreign to Hawai'i. It came already formed, already constituted as an international, imperialistic framework of commerce based on money economies, market systems, and organized production and exchange—all embedded in the ideological assumptions of nation-state systems of government and Christian morality.[3] In its penetration of Hawai'i, capitalism encountered a radically different social structure in the total sense of that Marxist–Althusserian concept. From the late 1700s and throughout the 1800s, Hawaiian history revolved around the conjuncture and articulation of capitalism and the two coexisting Hawaiian modes of production—the dominant hierarchical mode and the communal mode. In this intersection of histories and structures, the contradictions of all three modes of social organization became apparent.

Both "tragic" and "comedic" emplotments of Hawai'i's history tend to present the West as a monolithic force that simply moved into Hawai'i and changed it. This view masks the contra-

dictions that existed within Western social structures and contending social forces present within Western societies, particularly in the United States, where serious threats to national unity
were not resolved until the mid-1800s and the conclusion of the
Civil War. It is also a view that contains assumptions of Western
superiority and Hawaiian inferiority, assumptions that justified
imperialism in the nineteenth century and rationalized continuing exploitation into the twentieth century. It is a legacy of the
ideology that American domination was part of the inevitable
march of civilization and progress, with political and economic
ambitions masked and legitimized in a discourse of Manifest Destiny—a divine plan that ordered and justified American expansion
into the Pacific as far away as the Philippines.

Although capitalism in the nineteenth century did have a structural coherency strong enough to operate as a global system, it was
not as tightly structured as the corporate capitalism that exists
today. The United States had not yet consolidated and established
its control over the mainland; at the same time that American
entrepreneurs were trying to establish a foothold for trade in
Hawai'i, the American government was fighting to consolidate its
political control over the western half of the country through policies of settlement, conquest, and appropriation—the construction of railroads, the settlement of land, the extermination or
reterritorialization of American Indians, and the discursive construction of a sense of national unity through a rhetoric of the
"Americanization" of the frontier.[4]

A major qualitative difference arising from the exogenous nature of capitalism in Hawai'i has to do with "culture." In Europe,
capitalism developed out of changes in the relations and forces
of production, with related structural changes occurring in the
political and ideological instances as modern nation-states took
shape. The rationalization of science and the secularization of
societies during the Enlightenment challenged the dominance
of religion, the ideological level losing the position of structural
dominance it held under feudalism. But while the emergence

of capitalism marked a fundamental change in European social structures, it was not accompanied by a complete reconstruction of the forms and content of ideological practices and cultural systems as it was in Hawai'i. In Hawai'i, as in other societies penetrated by Western imperial power, the structural shift to capitalism involved major transformations in the ideological arenas of religion, language, and knowledge, and introduced new symbolic forms and practices of social representation.

The Penetration of Capitalism

The antagonism between capitalism and the two Hawaiian modes of production became evident during the middle of the 1800s when wage labor, a monetary-based system of exchange, and private landownership became generalized in the islands. A period of transition preceded that time. In the early years, there was only intermittent trade; in the later transition years, Western trade, centered on sandalwood, dominated the Hawaiian hierarchical mode of production. When Hawai'i and the West met for the first time in 1778, Hawai'i had no currency: goods moved through a system of tribute from *maka'āinana* to *mō'ī* up the hierarchical ladder and through in-kind exchange among the *maka'āinana*. The economy was based on agriculture and fishing, both well developed and highly intensified. Land, which was the material manifestation of power, was held by the *mō'ī* of the island (or island district) and distributed among his *ali'i* supporters for their use and management.

Early Interactions: Recoding Cultural Categories

Until roughly 1815, there was only occasional commerce and interaction between the majority of Hawaiians and Westerners. Trade was on an in-kind basis with Hawaiians supplying produce and sometimes the "favors" of women in exchange for iron and other Western goods, primarily with fur traders. Daily life was little affected for most Hawaiians by this early trade, although even these infrequent interactions between Westerners and Hawaiians were important for their impact on the ideological coherency of the Hawaiian social structure. During the War of 1812 between the United States and Britain, visits by fur traders decreased, but the pace of exchange picked up again in 1815 with the close of the war and the end of the British blockade of American ports, only to dwindle gradually as other areas of trade became more profitable for the West.[5] At this point, Kamehameha I's conquest and unification of the islands had a greater structural impact than early interactions and relations with outsiders. The structural changes that Kamehameha initiated—the centralization of religious, political, and economic institutions and changes in chiefly land tenure—ended the structured cycles of wars, consolidation, and usurpation. More important, his acts, which were intended to strengthen his own power, had the unintended consequence of weakening the power of later Hawaiian kings.[6]

Even though the early fur trade was relatively minor in terms of its economic impact, underlying ideological codes that legitimized the hierarchical structure were put in jeopardy by these early interactions between Hawaiians and Westerners. Sahlins characterizes Hawaiian culture as performative and flexible within its structure of cultural categories, an ongoing synthesis of stability and change, production and transformation.[7] During the initial period of contact, Hawaiian responses to the new situations posed by the presence of Westerners were shaped by existing cultural categories. For instance, Cook's arrival was integrated into the Hawaiian tradition that the high and powerful come from the outside. He was perceived by Hawaiians as someone extremely powerful, perhaps as a god, at the very least as an important foreign chief.[8]

As interaction with Westerners increased into the 1800s and new material practices replaced old ones (particularly those that violated *kapu*, such as women eating with men, or that broke relationships of production between *ali'i* and *maka'āinana*, such as when the latter left their agricultural tasks to sign on with trading ships), traditional social structures were altered, and received cultural categories were incapable of coding a new, complex reality. The meanings of practices, forms, events, places, and people changed accordingly.[9] The basic categories of gender and sexuality were transformed by intercourse (eating and bartering as well as sexual) between Hawaiian women and the men of the West. These new practices of sex and social relations jeopardized fundamental categories of what was sacred and what was defiling, relationships grounded in the fundamental concepts of *mana, kapu,* and *noa.* Brad Shore points out that because *mana* was linked to generative potence, it had a "special relationship to the two primary sources of human life: food and sex."[10] Therefore, Western–Hawaiian interactions that violated *kapu* dealing with male–female eating practices and sex had immense ideological and therefore political implications for the Hawaiian social structure. These new practices resulted in new valuations of gender and sexual activity. The sexuality of Hawaiians, which had been religiously constituted and a source of *mana* and enjoyment, was devalued religiously (sex as sin) and revalued as commerce (sex as trade).[11] According to Sahline,

> This passionate commerce soon became an important means of the people's trade, with a view toward circumventing at once the priests' tabus and the chiefs' business. And when ordinary men found common interest with their women in tabu transgressions, it broke down their own sacral status as men in contrast to women. . . . But now the developing class cleavage revised the ancient proportions of tabu, making salient the radical opposition of ruling chiefs and common people. . . . This is a true structural transformation, a pragmatic redefinition of the categories that alters the relationships between them.[12]

Reordering Social Relationships

By 1830, a significant shift in power had taken place as the result of a confluence of several forces, including what Kamehameha I had done in terms of centralizing power and adopting Western technologies, the increasing numbers of outsiders seeking to exploit the resources of the islands for trade, Kamehameha II's and Ka'ahumanu's purposeful breach of eating *kapu* following the death of Kamehameha I in 1819, increasing disease and death for Hawaiians, and the arrival and influence of American missionaries. These forces and events constituted an overdetermination of contradictions that seriously jeopardized the existing social structure. In Althusser's words, they resulted in "an accumulation of 'circumstances' and 'currents' so that whatever their origin and sense . . . they 'fuse' into a *ruptural unity.*"[13]

By 1810, the sandalwood trade had become economically and socially significant. The practices associated with this trade impinged on the totality of Hawaiian social relations and material production in ways that interactions with fur traders had not.[14] As Kent makes clear, the sandalwood trade was part of an international global market. Not wanting to deplete their supplies of gold and silver, British and American traders looked for something to trade to the Chinese in return for the tea, silk, and spices that were in great demand in Europe and the United States. Sandalwood, which grew in Hawai'i and was desired by the Chinese for making fans and ornaments, was the answer to their problems. The very considerable profit for traders who bartered silk, carriages, and other Western luxury items for sandalwood in Hawai'i, which was traded for Chinese goods that were sold in the West, resulted in a relatively short but intense and structurally significant period of trade in Hawai'i.

Kamehameha I's political victories vis-à-vis other Hawaiian high chiefs in part reflected his ability to control economic and political relations with Westerners.[15] After his death, subordinate *ali'i* who had acted as his agents entered into individual contracts with Western traders, supplying sandalwood in return for highly desired Western goods, which became new symbols of status. To meet their contracts, *ali'i* diverted the *maka'āinana* (already suffering from Western-introduced diseases) from agricultural production, sending them into the mountains for wood. Not only was this extremely hard on the *maka'āinana* physically, it seriously disrupted agricultural production, resulting in shortages of food. The extraction of sandalwood could not keep up with the contractual commitments of the *ali'i*; by the middle of the 1820s, they had accumulated staggering debts to foreign traders and the growing number of local merchants.

The sandalwood trade declined in the mid-1820s as the *ali'i* became disillusioned and indebted and as the quality of the wood decreased. American traders, who began to fear they would never be paid, succeeded in 1826 in getting the American navy to pressure Kamehameha III to acknowledge these debts as government debts. To pay them, the Hawaiian government required all Hawaiians to deliver, within nine months, "half a picul of good sandalwood, or in lieu of sandalwood, four Spanish dollars or any valuable commodity worth that amount." In return, each man was permitted to cut half a picul for himself as well. Women were required to furnish *tapa* mats of equal value, or one Spanish dollar. Only the stimulus of these debts kept the sandalwood trade going between 1827 and 1830. But the *ali'i* were unable to pay what they had borrowed, as well as the ever-mounting interest on the debts. In fact, *ali'i* continued to incur new debts as traders and merchants extended credit to stimulate sales. Eventually the sandalwood was gone, but the debts remained, a source of contention between *ali'i*, the Hawaiian government, and Western traders until 1843, when the debts were finally paid off.

Even after the formal religious–political structures of Hawai'i were abolished in 1819 by Kamehameha II and the powerful consort, Ka'ahumanu, the structured relations of production and distribution between *ali'i* and *maka'āinana* remained intact for another decade or so. The old relations of production and distribution continued to exist as long as traditional practices of in-kind exchange among the *maka'āinana* and tribute between *maka'āinana* and *ali'i* continued, particularly where such practices operated within long-established land-based relations of production managed by *konohiki*.[16] But during the period of frantic trade in sandalwood after Kamehameha I's death, *ali'i* used their privileges of *kapu* in unprecedented ways. Their unreasonable demands on the *maka'āinana* stripped away the still-remaining vestiges of religious meaning from practices of tribute. Structural contradictions arising from relations of domination could no longer be legitimized or masked by the political–religious ideology of the hierarchical social structure.

Throughout the sandalwood era, the capitalist mode of production exploited the Hawaiian hierarchical mode of production with Western traders working through the *ali'i* and their positions of authority within the tributory structure to exploit the full economic potential of the sandalwood forests.[17] In effect, this trade in raw resources was integrated into the reproduction of the hierarchical mode of production. But when trade moved to goods that could be gotten directly from *the maka'āinana*, the political and economic powers of the *ali'i* were undercut. With money as the medium of exchange (rather than sandalwood traded for goods), the capitalist mode of production became dominant. A capitalist social formation then moved to the fore, completely effacing the hierarchical mode of production. Because of the relative indifference of commoners to wage incentives, however, the communal mode of production survived through the nineteenth century and into the twentieth, long after the last vestiges of the hierarchical social structure had vanished.

Historical accounts of this era often characterize the *ali'i* as "greedy," as willing dupes of Western traders, or both, and the *maka'āinana* as too ignorant or apathetic to resist their treatment.[18] The imputation of good or evil or willful manipulation or irresponsible behavior ignores Hawaiian cultural categories of *mana*, status and hierarchy. The *ali'i* and the *maka'āinana*, as well as Western traders and missionaries, were acting within the "imagined realities" of their respective social structures, and in that context their responses to contact "made sense." For the *ali'i*, with land no longer the index of power that it had been before Kamehameha I's establishment of a central government, Western goods became new symbols of chiefly status, new indicators of *mana*. Borofsky and Howard similarly question the suitability of the Western concept of "theft" to characterize Polynesians' attempts to take objects from the boats of Cook and other early explorers. They argue that such actions are better understood in terms of Hawaiian ways of negotiating status rather than Western notions of property and morality.[19]

Godelier emphasizes the necessity for those trying to understand the rationality of any social system and the behaviors of people inscribed by it to focus on structures and meanings.

> When Westerners see irrational behavior, the explanation is not to be sought in the "bizarre" psychology of the individuals and peoples concerned, but in the logic of the traditional social relations, in the hierarchy of these relations. It is this hierarchy that provides the basis for the "social necessity, social utility," of a particular category of goods, a particular form of activity.[20]

After the demise of the sandalwood trade in the 1830s, the whaling industry dominated trade and commerce in Hawai'i. Located within one of the three principal whaling areas of the Pacific, Hawai'i became a major base for New England whalers to refit, reprovision, and relax. This trade was not based on large-scale extraction of raw resources (as with sandalwood), but on exchange for food, goods, and services. The *ali'i* were no longer needed as middlemen between Western traders and *maka'āinana*; instead whalers and traders dealt directly with the latter for food and incidental labor around the harbors and in the small towns around them. As a result, *ali'i* were increasingly marginalized, their wealth based in tracts of land that had little capital value under the system of land tenure that still existed. Of course, that was soon to change with the *Māhele*.

Hawai'i's political-economy was subject to developments and practices generated by the larger arena of international trade. Fluctuations in whaling activity responded to increases and decreases in whale-oil prices on the international market, to depressions in the U.S. economy, and finally to the almost total disappearance of whaling because of the increasing use of petroleum and the near-total destruction of the whaling fleet in the ice floes of the North Pacific in 1871. The whaling trade was at its peak during the 1840s and 1850s; between 1845 and 1854, approximately forty-eight hundred whaling ships docked in Honolulu and Lahaina, close to 90 percent of them American owned.[21] In addition to whaling, this period saw a considerable amount of general trade with settlements on the west coast of the U.S. mainland, and with other Pacific islands for which Honolulu served as a trading center. By the 1870s, when the whaling trade ended, sugar had already emerged as the centerpiece of a new capitalist economy.

Transformation to Capitalism: The *Māhele*

In the 1840s and 1850s, several key structural events significantly affected the material practices and basic structure of the islands. These events changed the daily lives of Hawaiians, causing many to leave the land and even the islands and causing further disruption to traditional patterns of social, political, and economic relationships. One such structural event was the passing of tax laws. In 1841, commoners were required to pay tax either in currency or in labor, half of the tax going to the "landlord" whose land they lived on and half to the king or government. The Penal Code of 1850, however, was more far-reaching in its structural impact, for it required that taxes be paid in currency. This forced Hawaiians living on the land to enter the market economy, either as wage laborers or as sellers of agricultural products. The latter was a viable alternative during the 1850s, but by the end of the 1860s the agricultural market had collapsed with the demise of the whaling industry. This meant that, for the majority of Hawaiians, there was little alternative to wage labor.[22]

But the major economic event affecting the underlying structure of the Hawaiian social system was the change in the system of land tenure. Although the king's traditional right to be the sole determiner of land allocation had been modified by the 1839 Declaration of Rights, which stated that property could not be taken from anyone "except by express provision of the laws,"[23] until the 1850s foreigners could not buy land or even secure long-term leases. Instituting a system of private property had been a major goal for Western business interests in Hawai'i for a number of years, as they perceived private landownership a necessary condition for capital investment, particularly for large-scale investment in plantation agriculture. The American missionaries, who were so influential in affecting government policy, argued for a system of private ownership on the grounds that it would provide capitalist incentives to Hawaiians as well as the security of owning their own land.

The government's first concession had been a fifty-year lease given to Ladd and Company in 1835 for an experimental attempt to grow sugar on Kaua'i.[24] This lease whetted the appetite of other foreigners for land, if not through ownership, at least through similar long-term leases. Finally, in the 1840s, Kamehameha III began to listen to the urgings of his *haole* advisers, most notably Dr. Gerrit P. Judd and William Richards, both former missionaries who had resigned from the Mission Board when they became advisers to the king and his cabinet. First, Kamehameha III agreed to additional fifty-year leases; finally, to outright ownership of land. A commission was set up to devise a system of land division.

A number of Hawaiians expressed their growing concern about the influence of foreign advisers and the political and economic changes they saw taking place. In 1845, a petition with sixteen hundred names was sent to Kamehameha III from "the common people of your kingdom." It began:

> To His Majesty Kamehameha III and the Premier Kehauluahi, and all the Hawaiian Chiefs in council assembled: on account of our anxiety, we petition you, the father of the Hawaiian kingdom, and the following is our petition.
> 1. Concerning the independence of your kingdom.
> 2. That you dismiss the foreign officers whom you have appointed to be Hawaiian officers.
> 3. We do not wish foreigners to take the oath of allegiance and become Hawaiian subjects.
> 4. We do not wish you to sell any more land pertaining to your kingdom to foreigners.
> 5. We do not wish taxes in a confused obscure manner to be imposed in your kingdom.
> 6. This is the cause of our wishing to dismiss these foreign officers.[25]

The Commodification of Land

This and similar petitions were ignored. The result of the land commission's work was the *Māhele* of 1848, which separated the lands of the kingdom into those of the king (60 percent) and 250 chiefs and *konohiki* (39 percent). The king's lands were further divided into his own private lands (Crown Lands) and Government Lands. The result was that approximately one million acres became Crown Lands, one and half million became Government Lands, and another one and a half million went to *ali'i*. Less than 1 percent, or 30,000 acres of land, went to commoners. To rectify this, in 1849 the land commission was empowered to give commoners title to their *kuleana* if they filed a legal claim.

The *Kuleana* Act that was passed in 1850 gave commoners the opportunity to acquire title to land they and their families had worked, as well as the right to continue to acquire firewood, timber, and water from surrounding lands held by *ali'i*. In addition, and most important, resident aliens were permitted to acquire and sell land. In 1850, Judge Lee, speaking to the Hawaiian Agricultural Society, whose *haole* members benefited enormously from the *Māhele*, applauded the new capitalist system of property ownership for what it would do for the commoners:

> Until the past year the Hawaiian held his land as a mere tenant at will, subject to be dispossessed at any time it might suit the will or caprice of his chief or that of his more oppressive luna. Of what avail was it to the common people to raise more than enough to supply the immediate wants of their subsistence? Would the surplus belong to them. . . . Far from it. It would go to swell the stores of their despotic lords, who claimed an absolute right in all their property, and who periodically sent forth their hordes of *lunas* to scour the country and plunder the people without the shadow of right or mercy. Often these ravagers, their *land-pirates* leave the poor *makaainana* (peasant) with little else than his *malo*, his digger and his calabash. I thank God that these things are at an end, and that the poor Kanaka may now stand on the border of his little taro-patch, and holding his fee-simple title in his hand, bid defiance to the world.[26]

But the system of land titles that originated in the *Māhele* involved a concept of land as property that was totally alien to Hawaiians, particularly the *maka'āinana*, who had used land for sustenance and for tributary payments. Although they had had no formalized rights to permanent land tenure under the hierarchical mode of production, a *kuleana* was usually worked by generations of the same family. Under the new laws, commoners were required to file claims for land they were occupying and cultivating, and then give supporting testimony. Many did not do this, failing to complete the complicated legal steps or lacking the fees necessary to file. Some who initiated action on their claims died before the process, which could take several years, was completed, as this was a time of four devastating epidemics: measles, whooping cough, diarrhea, and influenza. These epidemics killed more than ten thousand people in a twelve-month period; the overwhelming majority of those who died were Hawaiians.[27] The Hawaiian population dropped between 1850 and 1853 at a rate of 3.5 percent annually, from about eight-five thousand to seventy-one thousand. Roughly 10 percent of the people claiming land in 1848 had died by 1854.[28]

Some *maka'āinana* who obtained titles to their land found they could not pay the annual land taxes or sustain themselves on their small plots of land because, in spite of the intent of the *Kuleana* Act, under the new system of land as exclusive property, Hawaiians no longer had access to the full range of land-based resources that had been available to them under the old system. The *Māhele* thus put an end to the traditional system of land management that had made both the communal and the tribute-based systems of production and distribution viable. In the process of this restructuring of land holding and use, irrigation systems deteriorated, agricultural production fell, and, most important, the relatively affluent subsistence existence that the *maka'ainana* had enjoyed ended.

By 1886, two-thirds of all government-allotted land was owned by foreigners.[29] Amos Cooke, a missionary who ran the Chief's Children's School and who later became a partner in what was to be one of the major sugar-producing and land-holding companies of the islands, Castle and Cooke, expressed the following thoughts about the divine destiny of Hawaiians and their lands:

It seems as if Providence was fighting against the nation internally (for it has always appeared as if Providence was contending against other nations). Diseases are fast numbering the people with the dead and many more are slow to take advantage of the times and of the privileges granted to them by the King and Government (as you will learn in the Polynesian). While the natives stand confounded and amazed at their privileges and doubting the truth of the changes on their behalf, the foreigners are creeping in among them, getting their largest and best lands, water privileges, building lots, etc., etc. The Lord seems to be allowing such things to take place that the Islands may gradually pass into other hands. This is trying but we cannot help it. It is what we have been contending against for years, but the Lord is showing us that His thoughts are not our thoughts, neither are His ways our ways. The will of the Lord be done.[30]

Therefore, a host of social and economic factors—unpayable taxes, unproductive land allocations, unfamiliar legal requirements necessary to secure titles, tempting sums of money offered by land speculators, disease and death—caused many Hawaiians, *maka'āinana* and *ali'i*, to relinquish their land, selling it or simply leaving it. In effect, instead of securing land for Hawaiians, as the missionaries had hoped and so convincingly argued, the *Māhele* alienated Hawaiians from the land.

The Proletarianization of Hawaiians

With the institution of private property and wage labor, Hawaiians were increasingly drawn into the cash economy as wage laborers. Many were hired as ship hands or to work on the west coast of the mainland; others took menial jobs in the towns; some worked on plantations. "In the face of a multitude of factors acting to drive them from the land, the ultimate fate of most Hawaiians was proletarianization."[31] The proletarianization of the Hawaiians (*ali'i* as well as *maka'āinana*) was apparent in the growing urbanization of Honolulu as Hawaiians left the land to find wage-paying jobs with the growing number of permanent or semipermanent resident merchants and shopkeepers that had set up trade there. As the market economy developed, it in turn generated local demands for consumption goods. Hawai'i was no longer simply a place to extract raw goods but a market for imported goods. In Honolulu, wage labor (the commodification of time) and housing (the commodification of space) articulated with the marketing of products. The result was the rapid growth of Honolulu as the economic and political center of the islands. Of the two modes of production of precontact Hawai'i (the hierarchical and the communal), only the earlier communal mode of production continued to function on the margins of the capitalist economy, primarily in rural areas of the islands. Even to the present, the ideology and practices of that older mode of production are culturally important, still evident in Hawaiian practices of sharing among the *'ohana*—a now more broadly defined term of family and community relationships.[32] With the transformation to capitalism, Hawai'i was more fully integrated into the international market system. The mediation and transformation of a monetary-based system of equivalency produced cycles of exchange that pulled labor, products, land, and capital into relations of global trade and finance that extended far beyond the islands. Sugar, the driving force of this global trade, would dominate the economy and the politics of the islands for the next hundred years.

The New Political-Economy of Sugar

Private ownership of land allowed the formation of large land holdings, which made large-scale sugar production feasible. Again, land became a mechanism of social mobilization and organization, but under a totally new system of production wherein agriculture became an industry dominated by capital, rather than production articulated by religion, status politics, and communal needs. With a system of private property in place, Hawai'i was finally "ready" for full-scale capitalism. Investment could now be focused on meeting the demands of the United States for sugar, production of sugar in the South having been seriously disrupted by the American Civil War. With land secured and a sugar market on the mainland, all that was needed for maximum profitability was cheap labor and a favorable trade agreement with the United States.

In the early days of the sugar economy, Hawaiians constituted four-fifths of the plantation workforce (2,627 out of a total of 3,786 in 1873). But the Hawaiian population was decreasing in number and insufficient to meet the large labor needs of the plantations.[33] The labor problem was solved with the importation of contract labor from several countries, in large numbers first from China and then from Japan and the Philippines, where peasants and workers were eager to escape extremely adverse social and economic conditions.[34] Other immigrants from Europe, the Pacific, and elsewhere in Asia came to Hawai'i to work. The profitability of sugar was finally secured in 1876 when the U.S. Congress and the Hawaiian legislature passed enabling acts for the Reciprocity Treaty, which allowed Hawaiian sugar to enter the United States duty free, thereby making Hawaiian sugar competitive with other sources of sugar.

As both labor and property became increasingly commodified in Hawai'i, economic production was underwritten by the ideological discourses and practices of New England Protestantism and American notions of individualism and government. The Hawaiian kings and their governments were increasingly dominated by economic interests that depended on the continued growth of sugar. The largely Western-styled government's role became one of providing needed services and infrastructure, such as building harbor facilities for sugar export and constructing railroads to move sugar from rural areas to the docks. In addition, the government was actively involved in the reproduction of labor and relations of production. This was evident in the efforts of King Kalākaua and his government to negotiate with other countries for labor and in the use of the state apparatus to legislate labor laws beneficial to the sugar plantation owners and enforce the Masters and Servants Act of 1850 that controlled labor conditions until U.S. annexation of the islands in 1898. The growing bureaucratization of the government apparatus in the last quarter of the nineteenth century can be seen in Thrum's *Hawaiian Almanacs and Annuals*. Tables in these annuals show increasing government outlays for government workers and physical infrastructures that primarily supported sugar production and related commerce.[35]

As the sugar industry developed, so did the ranks of labor. Although labor and capital are interdependent under capitalism, the relationship is a source of contradiction and conflict. Certainly Hawaiians and Asian contract laborers resented the oppression of the plantation system. Open conflicts between sugar growers and workers were averted for a time by the importation of successive groups of indentured workers. Many plantation managers purposefully worked ethnic group against ethnic group, using cultural and language differences to forestall the development of labor solidarity. In the early years of the industry, conflicts between owners and workers were labeled as worker intractability, labor-contract problems, and disputes over living and working conditions. Not until the twentieth century were these conflicts translated into larger issues of politics, power, and class.

Hawaiian Sovereignty at Risk

As sugar became the mainstay of the islands' economy, Hawaiian control and sovereignty were increasingly jeopardized. A Hawaiian nationalist movement began in the 1870s, marshaling Hawaiians under the slogan "Hawaii for Hawaiians." Feeling their economic and political control threatened, the *haole* elite turned on Kalākaua and became very vocal in their criticism of his style of government. They wrote newspaper editorials castigating his "extravagant" expenditures on the 'Iolani Palace, on his coronation and birthday jubilee, and other perceived evidences of his unfitness to rule. But the major point of controversy was Kalākaua's opposition to the ceding of Pearl Harbor to the United States in return for the renewal of the Reciprocity Treaty, which had expired in 1886. To get their way on this and other matters affecting their position in the islands, members of the economic and political elite (second-generation missionary families, plantation owners,

sugar and trade agents) forced Kalākaua to sign a new constitution that greatly limited the powers of the monarchy. The "Bayo-
net Constitution" of 1887, the same year the Reciprocity Treaty
was renewed and the United States acquired exclusive rights to
Pearl Harbor, was the primary focus of Hawaiian dissatisfaction
until Kalākaua's death in 1891. Realizing that Queen Lili'uokalani
would continually oppose their plans for economic and political
expansion, the Americans organized and eventually effected, in
1893, the overthrow of the Hawaiian monarchy backed up by the
threat of American marines. A provisional government was set
up, followed by a republic in 1894 and annexation in 1898—the
same period in which the United States acquired Cuba, Puerto
Rico, Guam, the Philippines, and the Virgin Islands as a result
of the Spanish-American War. The result of annexation was the
total appropriation of the Hawaiian islands by American economic and political interests.[36]

   With the arrival of Cook and Western economic and political
interests, the tightly articulated social structure of the islands
began to shift, separate, and disintegrate. As trade-for-money inserted itself into the daily lives of the Hawaiians, as land became
capital, as wages replaced in-kind exchange and distribution, the
lives of Hawaiians changed radically. With material practices of
all kinds—political, religious, and economic—drastically altered,
old Hawaiian metaphors could no longer read the new reality.
Hawaiian alienation was intensified by the devastation of disease,
death, and infertility. The Hawaiian population continued to decline through 1872, reaching a low of approximately fifty-seven
thousand. Not until the census of 1878, one year after the Reciprocity Treaty, did the total population of the islands level off and
begin to rise with the immigration of imported labor.[37]

   Processes of social alienation and ideological reconstitution
take place wherever one culture colonizes another. In many ways,
however, the history of Hawai'i is unique in the annals of imperialism. Here was a society that went from chiefly enclaves to

British-style monarchy to pseudo republic to annexed territory to U.S. state—all over the course of a century and a half. In the second half of the twentieth century, while colonies throughout the world were regaining their independence, Hawai'i irrevocably lost its sovereignty when it was incorporated as the fiftieth state of the United States. As the Hawaiian social formation was transformed, a new hegemony began to take shape. Western ideologies eclipsed Hawaiian ideologies, and new Western forms or Western-influenced forms of expression replaced old ones. The politics of culture was played out in many arenas during the nineteenth century; one of these arenas was Hawaiian music. In the next chapter, we take a closer look at how ideology and forms of social representation changed with the political and economic restructuring of the islands.

Dance des hommes dans les Iles Sandwich, painted by Louis Choris, a landscape artist on the *Rurick*, a Russian ship captained by Otto von Kotzebue, which visited Hawai'i in 1816. Hawaii State Archives

Arago, an artist on the French warship *L'Uranie,* which visited Hawai'i in 1819, called this *Iles Sandwich: Maisons de Karaimoku.* It is a "typical landscape" painted for an avid European public, combining realism and romanticism. Hawaii State Archives

Jeune femme des îles Sandwich dansant.

Arago's depiction of a young woman dancing a sitting *hula*. One year before the missionaries arrived, Arago wrote, "Let us . . . leave these good people to their early habits and inclinations. . . . Why teach them desires and wants? If repose, comfort, tranquillity and pleasure constitute happiness, they are happy." Hawaii State Archives

Hawaiian dance has been a spectacle for the foreign gaze since early contact; this party for the officers and crew of the French warship *La Bonité* in the fall of 1836 was painted by the ship's artist, B. Lauvergne. Although "missionary rule" was being challenged at this time, *hula* dancers were still well covered. Hawaii State Archives

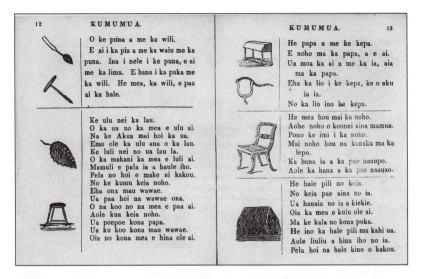

O ke puna a me ka wili.
E ai i ka pia a me ka waiu me ka
puna. Ina i nele i ke puna, e ai
me ka lima. E hana i ka puka me
ka wili. He mea, ka wili, e paa
ai ka hale.

Ke ulu nei ka lau.
O ka ua no ka mea e ulu ai.
Na ke Akua mai hoi ka ua.
Emo ole ka ulu ana o ka lau.
Ke luli nei no ua lau la.
O ka makani ka mea e luli ai.
Mamuli e pala ia a haule iho.
Pela no hoi e make ai kakou.
No ke kumu keia noho.
Eha ona mau wawae.
Ua paa hoi na wawae ona.
O na koo no na mea e paa ai.
Aole kua keia noho.
Ua poepoe kona papa.
Ua ku koo kona mau wawae.
Oia no kona mea e hina ole ai.

He papa a me ke kepa.
E noho ma ka papa, a e ai.
Ua moa ka ai a me ka ia, aia
ma ka papa.
Eha ka lio i ke kepa, ke o aku
ia ia.
No ka lio ino ke kepa.

He mea hou mai ka noho.
Aohe noho o koonei aina mamua.
Pono ke imi i ka noho.
Mai noho hou na kanaka ma ka
lepo.
Ka hana ia a ka poe naaupo.
Aole ka hana a ka poe naauao.

He hale pili no keia.
No keia pae aina no ia.
Ua hanaia no ia a kiekie.
Oia ka mea e kulu ole ai.
Ma ke kala no kona puka.
He ino ka hale pili ma kahi ua.
Aole liuliu a hina iho no ia.
Pela hoi na hale kino o kakou.

Sheldon Dibble, a missionary who translated many books for the Mission Press between 1832 and 1840, prepared this edition of the primer *Mea Pa'i Palapala a Na Misionari* in 1837. Offering the power of literacy, it also teaches the superiority of Western civilization. For example, this text introduces the chair, stating that ignorant people sit on dirt but intelligent people do not. Bishop Museum

Kinaʻu, regent and ardent Christian convert, and her attendants returning from church in 1837. It is an interesting juxtaposition of *muʻumuʻu*-clad Hawaiian royal women, Western observers, and natives being flogged. At the time, tension ran high between French representatives, Hawaiian rulers, and American missionaries over the presence of Catholic priests in Hawaiʻi. The artist, J. Masselot, was on the French frigate *La Vénus*, whose captain, Abel du Petit Thouars, intervened on behalf of French priests. Hawaii State Archives

A missionary preaching to Hawaiians in a Kukui grove on Kauai, by A. T. Agate, who accompanied the U.S. Exploring Expedition led by Charles Wilkes, 1840–1841. By 1845, artists' renderings of the landscape and people of the Pacific were displaced by photography as the preferred representational medium of science. Hawaii State Archives

From 'Iolani Palace grounds looking toward the Music Hall, which opened in 1881 with a theatrical performance by a California theater company. Aliiolani Hale, where the legislature met, is on the left, with Honolulu harbor in the background. Hawaii State Archives

On the grounds of ʻIolani Palace, dancers perform for King Kalākaua's fiftieth Birthday Jubilee, November 16, 1886. For many Hawaiians chants and *hula* were statements of Hawaiian pride and sovereignty. However, to John L. Stevens, the American Minister to Hawaiʻi who supported the overthrow of the monarchy, the Jubilee performances were "a relic of a barbarism well forgotten." Hawaii State Archives

Following annexation in 1898, Honolulu grew at a rapid rate. This photograph of an active downtown street, taken around 1910, shows curbs and sidewalks, streetcars and horse-drawn carriages, streetlights, electrical lines, and telephone poles. Hawaii State Archives

Asians, brought to Hawai'i to work on the sugar plantations, were a significant presence in Honolulu by the end of the century. Frank Davey took this photograph in Chinatown just prior to the January 1900 fire set by the Fire Department on orders of the Board of Health to control an epidemic of bubonic plague. Hawaii State Archives

A studio sitting of exotic Hawaiian girls in *hula* attire, taken around 1890, long after dancers were prohibited from performing bare breasted. Identified as "probably taken by J. Williams," a popular photographer who worked in Honolulu from 1880 to about 1920. Hawaii State Archives

Somber, heavily clad Hawaiian chanters and dancers perform for a well-dressed *haole* audience in the early 1900s, not long after the annexation of the islands by the United States. Hawaii State Archives

An early example of tourist industry appropriation of *hula*. Here *haole* women, probably tourists, with Hawaiian women are "learning to *hula*." The photographer, L. E. Edgeworth, worked in Hawai'i between 1925 and 1929. Eaton Magoon Collection, Hawaii State Archives

Sheet music from 1934, when the Hawaiian music craze was sweeping the world. The title and the stylized background of exotic primitiveness—a grass hut and swaying palm trees—frame the romanticized Western concept of beautiful "Hawaiian" women. Rudy Vallee was one of several popular crooners who performed "My Little Grass Shack," by Harry Owens and Johnny Noble, two famous producers and performers of *hapa haole* music in the 1930s. DeSoto Brown Collection

Hollywood publicity photo from *Song of the Islands*, 1942, which starred Betty Grable, Victor Mature, and Hilo Hattie. Here Grable and *haole* dancers in cellophane skirts perform Hollywood's version of Hawaiian *hula*. Many Hollywood movies of that era presented Hawai'i as a romantic paradise. De-Soto Brown Collection

Commercialized *hula* simplified in take-home instructional books. Popular with Hawai'i visitors during the 1940s and 1950s, these books, presenting *hula* as something that could be self-taught "in ten easy lessons," reduced it to movement without meaning and diminished Hawaiian culture. DeSoto Brown Collection

An ad from the mid-1950s that prefigures the tourist boom that came with statehood and jet travel in the 1960s. Only the style and number of tour buses—and the cost of an island tour— has changed for the approximately 7 million tourists who come to Hawai'i annually. DeSoto Brown Collection

The fiftieth anniversary of the Kodak Hula Show, 1987. It is claimed that only Disneyland and Disney World sell more film than this show-business version of Hawaiian and Polynesian culture. *Honolulu Advertiser*, David Yamada, photographer

Dancers from *kumu hula* Alicia Smith's *hālau 'O Na Maoli Pua* won the women's *kahiko* competition at the 1989 Merrie Monarch Festival. *Honolulu Advertiser*, Carl Viti, photographer

Dancers from Robert Cazimero's *Hālau Na Kamalei* took third place in men's *kahiko* and first place in *'auana* at the 1989 Merrie Monarch Festival. Members from this *hālau* are also shown in the cover photo. *Honolulu Advertiser*, Carl Viti, photographer

Hula Hālau ʻO Kamuela, led by *kumu hula* Paleka Leinaʻala Mattos and Edward Kunewa Mook of Waimanalo. Winners in the 1991 Merrie Monarch Festival, they perform their first-place *hula kahiko, He Maʻi No ʻIolani*. *Honolulu Advertiser*, Bruce Asato, photographer

Chapter Five

Transformations in Ideological
Representations: Chant and *Hula*

 From Western perspectives, the extension of empire is usually seen as one aspect of broader Euro-centered historical transformations: the Renaissance and mercantilism, industrialization and trade, consolidation of and competition among European nation-states, and development of a capitalist-dominated world system. From the perspectives of the colonized, the arrival of the West has always been a moment of violence and rupture. Certainly there were fundamental differences in relationships of power from being an exporter of Western capitalism and culture and being an unwilling recipient. The violence generated by imperialism and colonialism—whether the violence of brute force or the more subtle violence of commerce and the "civilizing" of natives—disrupted internal processes of social reproduction, including the creation and production of symbolic forms and practices.

Most theoretical conceptualizations of the relationships between history, society, and representation are grounded in European historical experience, Western texts, and Western ideas of art and aesthetics.[1] To the extent that Marxist theories of culture have referred at all to the rest of the world, it has usually been to show, comparatively, what makes capitalism and capitalist cultures so different.

As Hawaiians were suddenly forced into relationships with other cultures, other languages, and other epistemes of knowledge and discourse, the forces that had constituted the dynamic of Hawaiian history before Cook were radically displaced and replaced by Western forces of power and change. Before contact with the West, Hawai'i had been a tightly articulated social structure. Hawaiians shared a common language, religion, and system of knowledge, and the islands' inhabitants were linked by relatively efficient intra- and interisland communications. Although variations in dialects and traditions existed between islands, and even within the larger islands, a common culture inscribed all Hawaiians.[2] Within this culture, chant and *hula* were the ideological center and the primary reservoir of social knowledge and history. Their content, form, and production were integral to the reproduction of the hierarchical social structure. In this chapter we consider what happened to chant and *hula* as the islands were pulled into the alienating and, in some ways, liberating system of capitalism.

Cultural Interaction in Hawai'i

During the early days of interaction, Hawaiian and Western cultures were largely distinct and separate. But Hawaiian culture increasingly was dominated by the foreign culture of the West. The end of the nineteenth century was marked by intense political struggle as Hawaiians sought to protect their culture and identity and maintain Hawaiian sovereignty. The cultural interactions of Hawai'i with the West from the early nineteenth century on into the twentieth century have been typical of other colonized cultures.

Cultural interaction can take different courses and patterns: cultural exchange, cultural domination, and cultural imperialism. All three occurred in Hawai'i. The least threatening was cultural exchange, where Hawai'i and the West creatively integrated each other's forms into their own cultural expressions. The adoption and incorporation of the Western *'ukulele* and guitar into Hawaiian music is an example. Hawaiians learned to play the guitar from the Mexicans, Spanish, and Portuguese hired as cowboys. The Hawaiians retuned guitars by loosening or "slackening" the strings to accompany Hawaiian songs in a lower voice register.

In a reverse cultural exchange, Hawai'i contributed the sounds of the steel guitar to U.S. country and western music.

Cultural domination also occurred in the islands as Western ideas of morality and Western forms of culture were imposed on Hawaiians under conditions of political control. This cultural interaction was evident in Hawai'i throughout the nineteenth century, from the explicit suppression of *hula* to the more subtle, implicit devaluations of Hawaiian expressive arts and the institutionalization of English as the language of business, government, and instruction.

Cultural imperialism involves the transfer of money, cultural resources, or both from the dominated to the dominating culture. This cultural interaction was not evident in Hawai'i until early in the twentieth century when Hawaiian music was exploited for considerable profit by mainland record companies. Very little of the money from those early Hawaiian recordings ever found its way into the hands of local composers and musicians.[3]

There is relatively little information in English-language sources on the cultural forms and practices of Western and Hawaiian cultures in Hawai'i during the nineteenth century. The "historical event–great man" approach of most histories of Hawai'i largely ignore the producers and performers of "culture" (Hawaiians or Westerners).[4] Much of the information that is available comes from Western or Western-influenced sources and forms such as accounts of visitors, impressions of missionaries, early missionary newspapers published in Hawaiian or English, and, later, news accounts of social happenings printed in privately owned or government-run newspapers. These sources provide some idea of what was going on in Honolulu and Lahaina, but relatively little about the other islands or about rural areas of O'ahu and Maui. Most of the English-language accounts reported only happenings that seemed noteworthy to Western observers. Because newspapers were an imported Western form, even Hawaiian papers tended to reflect Western definitions of what constitutes social events. As the transformation of Hawai'i to a capitalist social structure continued throughout the 1900s, as Western culture became what Gramsci calls the "natural social authority," the perceptions of what was newsworthy about the two cultures changed, with proportionally less attention devoted to Hawaiian cultural forms and practices and more to Western.

The Intrusion of Western Culture

As much as they were able, Americans brought their cultural entertainments with them. At first, there were only the songs and musical instruments of the sailors; later, in the 1820s, the hymns and instruments of the missionaries. After the 1840s, particularly after the *Māhele* opened the door to large-scale capital investment in Hawai'i, the missionaries were joined by a growing number of resident traders and merchants, Western diplomatic representatives, and an increasing naval presence.

All "socially acceptable" elements of these groups were integrated into the "society" of Honolulu, drawn into the attempts of the Western residents (primarily American) to fashion a middle-class milieu for themselves and their families reminiscent of what they had left behind in New England. The center of this "culture" was the selective tradition of bourgeois Western culture: English literature and drama and European classical music, mixed with whatever contemporary American works were thought to be morally uplifting. These forms of Western culture were practiced in informal literary readings, activities of music groups, and amateur theatricals that were increasingly supplemented by "professional" productions as the century wore on.

Various accounts reveal a hodgepodge of Western entertainment in Honolulu by midcentury.[5] For instance, in 1847 a small theater, the Thespian, opened, staging British farces and light plays, reportedly charging $1 for seats in the boxes and half that amount for the pit. The king attended the "crowded opening night." A more substantial theater, the Royal Hawaiian, was built in 1848, financed by stockholders. A visiting Shakespearean troupe in the mid-1850s performed *Hamlet* and *Richard III* there; the king and the general population of Honolulu, Western and Hawaiian, attended these performances. In 1849 a Negro minstrel company performed for two weeks in Honolulu, and the first circus came the next year, followed by at least one circus a year thereafter. "High culture" was present in an amateur musical society formally organized in 1851, later reorganized and led by Henry Berger, the German military band leader hired by King Kalākaua to direct the Royal Hawaiian Band. On New Year's Day, 1881, the new Music Hall opened with a melodrama, "The Marble Heart," performed by a California theater company. The building was a two-story brick structure described as a "Thespian temple with four large proscenium boxes of a quasi-Hindu-Moorish type." The interior, which was quite lavish by Hawai'i standards, had "luxurious seats, a private entrance for King Kalakaua and retinue on the Waikiki side that led to the royal box on the left of the stage surmounted by a large gilt crown, red velvet curtains, the new, wonderful electric lights that illuminated the whole building and a complete stock of scenery and fixtures for the large stage." However, a large epidemic of smallpox forced the theater to close, and it was not until 1890 that it reopened with "The Mikado."[6]

As the white population on the mainland's west coast grew, and as steamship transportation improved, many traveling performers put Honolulu on their itineraries. Western cultural fare in Honolulu thus expanded rapidly toward the end of the century. From accounts in the newspapers and Thrum's *Annuals,* it seems that one could find in Honolulu almost as full a range and calendar of Western cultural entertainments, elite as well as popular, as in any U.S. seaboard town of comparable size. Some of this activity was an explicit attempt on the part of the American middle-class residents to bring culture to the islands. This was a local variation of a larger national movement to Americanize a diverse and increasingly economically divided population and to contain the social unrest resulting from economic dislocations caused by corporate

Changes in Hawaiian Chant and *Hula*

The structural transformation of Hawai'i during the nineteenth century resulted in changes in Hawaiian music. Traditional chant was displaced as the primary form of symbolic creation and performance and became an accompaniment for *hula;* and *hula* was transformed from an accompaniment of chant to a form independent of chant (although almost always accompanied by song). New forms of *hula* developed that combined Hawaiian and Western musical forms; and new forms of Hawaiian music evolved from Western music, first from missionary-introduced hymns and later from various styles of Western popular music.

Hawaiian chant and *hula* proved to be both vulnerable and resilient to Western influence. Eyewitness accounts by visitors in the late 1700s and early 1800s indicate that chant and *hula* were widely performed in various social contexts.[9] But with the arrival of the missionaries and their strong objections to the "licentious" *hula,* there was a rapid decline in its public practice—at least around missionary stations in the late 1820s and through most of the 1830s. Otto von Kotzebue, a captain of the Russian Imperial Navy, made two visits to Hawai'i in the mid-1820s at what appears to have been a key period in the ascendancy of the missionaries: the death of Liholiho (Kamehameha II) and the accession of Kauikeaouli as Kamehameha III. Substantial social and political changes had apparently occurred in the few months between Kotzebue's two visits: "The missionary Bengham [*sic*] found means to obtain such an acendency over the imperious Kahumanna [*sic*], and, through her, over the nation, that in the course of only seven months an entire change had taken place:— we might have imagined ourselves in a different country." Kotzebue facetiously observed that in the closing months of 1825, the streets, once so full of life, seemed dead and deserted. Games of all kinds were sternly prohibited, and "singing is a punishable offense; and the consummate profligacy of attempting to dance would certainly find no mercy."[10]

At this time the regent, Kaʻahumanu, a fervent Christian convert, was consolidating political power. Until her death in 1832, Kaʻahumanu, her family of Maui chiefs, and her missionary advisers constituted the center of political power, challenged only slightly and ineffectually by the "misbehavior" of the young Kauikeaouli and his friends, the Oʻahu governor, Boki, and other chiefs unhappy over Kaʻahumanu's social edicts, which they characterized as "mission rule."[11] After Kaʻahumanu's death, there was a brief period of resistance by Kauikeaouli, which took the form of drinking and traditional Hawaiian pastimes, including *hula* festivals—actions the missionaries labeled "deviant behavior." "Mission rule" resumed under the new regent, Kinaʻu, and *hula* was danced primarily in rural areas, where it was possible to escape the penalties of the edicts that banned it.[12]

After the 1840s, *hula* was performed again in the courts of the more independent Kamehameha kings, Alexander Liholiho (IV) and Lot Kamehameha (V), and particularly Kalākaua. These leaders encouraged *hula* for their own enjoyment and as a symbol of Hawaiian sovereignty. At Kalākaua's coronation, chant and *hula* were prominently featured, to the consternation of some foreigners as well as some converted Hawaiians. Kalākaua's actions were criticized as a waste of money and a sign of backwardness— "a retrograde step of heathenism and a disgrace to the age."[13] By the mid-1800s, the rapid and tragic decline of the Hawaiian population had to have been an important factor in the infrequency of chant and *hula* performance. The institutional bases of the *hula hālau*—the *aliʻi* and the priesthoods—no longer existed, and dancers of the various *hālau* had been decimated by disease and death. Nevertheless, just as the less institutionalized forms of Hawaiian religion survived after the abolition of the formal *kapu* system, particularly among the *makaʻāinana*, so *hula* continued in its less formalized forms, particularly in areas away from Honolulu.

The Transformation of Chant

Although we commonly categorize chant as music, it is more accurately defined as poetry that is chanted.[14] It was primarily the words of chant, even when accompanied by *hula*, that were central to its meaning: "Dance without poetry did not exist."[15] Traditional cosmological and genealogical chants were carefully memorized and passed from generation to generation (unless consciously changed for political purposes), but many chants were created to mark special events and to honor specific *ali'i* and their "rites of passage," their fertility, and their accomplishments as military leaders—manifestations of their *mana*.

The poetry of chant described the interrelations of nature, the gods, *ali'i*, *maka'āinana*, men and women. The forms and practices of chant legitimated the distribution of power, affirming the collective whole that was produced and reproduced through the lives of the *ali'i*, the living links with the Hawaiian sacred past. The *kaona* of chant—the multiple layers of meanings, some too sacred to speak—were infused by the ideological force of language and symbolic forms. This was an "overcoding of reality," in which certain signifiers and symbols became sacred and overloaded with meaning. The Hawaiians had prophets, but no canonical eschatology of a better afterlife. Instead, they enjoyed ontological certainty based on a glorious, seemingly unbroken history—the ideological task of chant. Chants, particularly those celebrating *ali'i*, were integral to the structure of religious–political power and the hierarchical arrangement of power. Chants invested relationships of domination with the ideology of *aloha*, normalizing the social order by tying *ali'i* into the sacred cosmologies and genealogies. In essence the highest rulers were the ideological center of the world.[16]

The chant form (within which were many styles) was radically reconstituted by the structural transformation of Hawai'i. The two structuring principles of chant—religion and language—were undermined by the penetration of Western culture. The religious system had been fractured even before the first company of missionaries arrived in 1820 by increasing violations of *kapu* by *ali'i* and *maka'āinana*; by Kamehameha I's efforts to consolidate his power through changes in the religious system and land distribution; by Liholiho's and Ka'ahumanu's deliberate violation of *kapu* prohibiting men and women from eating together; and by the defeat of Kūkā'ilimoku, the high priest who tried to protect important *heiau* from destruction.

The decreasing use of the Hawaiian language and the decline in chant production and performance went hand in hand with religious–political changes. As a result, successive generations of Hawaiians lost their facility in the creative use of Hawaiian. Young Hawaiians, who earlier might have been selected for training by priests as chanters, were not taught the subtle, layered meanings of Hawaiian poetry or instructed in the practices of chant composition and performance. The overthrow of the monarchy, the annexation of the islands by the United States, and the imposition of American education were all but fatal to the creation of traditional and even Western-influenced forms of poetry by Hawaiians over the next several generations. "Dispersed throughout the Islands, with no chiefly patron to look to, the composers of chants in the ancient manner and the masters of the meaning of the elevated poetic style no longer had a strong incentive to pass on their knowledge and attainments to the children. Literary Hawaiian began to rapidly disappear."[17] Still, for several decades after they had learned to read and write in Hawaiian, Hawaiians were composing chants and Western lyric poetry, writing stories and some novels, and writing down traditional Hawaiian narratives for younger Hawaiians and later generations. Many of these texts were published in Hawaiian-language newspapers.[18]

Kalākaua's reign (1874–1891) has been called the "first Hawaiian Renaissance" because of his attempts to revitalize chant and *hula* in an effort to "Keep Hawaii for the Hawaiians," a nationalist sentiment that had been growing in Hawai'i since the *Māhele* period. Kalākaua encouraged the preservation of old chants and the composition of new ones, composing chants himself in the new song form.[19] On one ceremonial occasion, five different *mele hula* were performed to honor Kalākaua. As evidence of the changes that had occurred in chant and *hula* by that time, Kaeppler notes that only one was an old chant, a *mele pahu*, the most elevated of all Hawaiian chant styles because of the use of a *pahu*, the sacred temple drum. The use of this chant, which Kalākaua had inherited, demonstrated his genealogical legitimacy—a matter of great concern to this elected king. It was the only chant at that occasion, according to Kaeppler, that exhibited the traditional allusive quality of Hawaiian poetry: "The other dances are 19th-century compositions in which the narrative potential of Hawaiian dance has been exploited to make the dance easier to understand to those who no longer understood the poetic subtlety of the Hawaiian language, for by Kalākaua's time English had become the medium of communication."[20]

The tenuous presence of formalized practices of chant in the late 1800s is evident in references to Kalākaua's attempts to assemble chanters for his coronation in 1883, his calling to Honolulu "all the old Hawaiians, men and women, who were known to still retain the knowledge of the ancient meles and hulas."[21] Kalākaua invited Dr. A. Marques, an amateur musicologist living in Honolulu, to observe the practicing and performing of chant and *hula* for the coronation. Twenty-five years later, Marques bemoaned the lack of good recording technology when these chanters had been assembled, stating that by 1914 very few Hawaiians had retained "any real and unadulterated knowledge of the old art."[22]

With Queen Lili'uokalani's overthrow in 1893, chant no longer had a political base. Solo chanting declined rapidly after that, with only a few chanters surviving into the twentieth century. Accompanying a 1924 *Honolulu Advertiser* article on the surviving chanters was a picture of seventeen elderly men, most of them from Kaua'i and the island of Hawai'i.[23] In the 1920s and 1930s,

Helen Roberts, one of the first American ethnomusicologists, and a number of local scholars associated with the Bishop Museum undertook to record and interview some of the remaining chanters of the Kalākaua era, including James Pālea Kapihenui Kuluwai-maka, a "professional" chanter at Kalākaua's court. These efforts attempted to record what were then perceived to be the last surviving artists of a dying cultural practice.[24]

The Transformation of Hula

As chant was transformed, so, necessarily, was *hula*. Before Western contact, *hula* supplemented the words of the chanted poem—literally a form of "poetry in motion."[25] The meanings of the movements of *hula* were contained in the poetic references of the chant, the total signification of any one performed *mele hula* a combination of words, voice, movement, instrumentation, ritual, social context, and content.

In the nineteenth century, as chant and *hula* were divorced from their traditional context, *hula* became a semiautonomous dance form and was increasingly deritualized in its practice. Even when performed with chant, *hula* gradually became the dominant element, body movements overshadowing the poetry and its poetic–religious concepts and connotations. As a result, the meaning of chant and *hula* changed for performers and audiences.

Even more than chant, *hula* was an abomination to the missionaries. For them, the spiritual was bodiless; there was no way that *hula*, a celebration of the body, could be reconciled with their Christian religious beliefs, certainly not the *hula maʻi* that honored the genitals of an *aliʻi* and his procreative *mana*. The near-naked Hawaiian body was an affront to the missionaries' notions of decency and civilization; their first offensive was to conceal its limbs and torso in clothing; the second was to prescribe and limit its movements. While the missionaries reluctantly accepted sex as a necessity of reproduction, they decried as evil any practice that might excite sexual desire—and the missionaries rightfully perceived *hula* as sexually exciting. It is ironic that Christian services in Hawai'i (e.g., Easter Sunrise Services at Punchbowl Cemetery) now often include *hula,* an appropriation of *hula* by the religion that once so fiercely denigrated it. This reversal indicates the power of Western culture in Hawai'i, desacralizing *hula* in the nineteenth century, resacralizing it in the twentieth. Ethnomusicologists have traced changes in *hula* and the new music that accompanied it during the nineteenth century, noting the incorporation of European harmony, instrumentation (primarily *'ukulele* and guitar), and even ballroom dance steps. New forms, called *hula noa* (free *hula*) because they were no longer restricted by the rituals and *kapu* of traditional Hawaiian practice, became increasingly popular; older, more demanding forms fell into disuse without the structure of *hula hālau,* the creative and religious leadership of composer priests, and the support and inspiration of *ali'i. Hula ku'i (ku'i* meaning to "join," a term for the new genre of *hula* and its accompanying music) was a conscious effort to combine old Hawaiian forms with Western forms. The *hula ku'i* was publicly acknowledged at Kalākaua's coronation in 1883, the ninth anniversary of his election as king, and performed at other court occasions during his reign, including his Fiftieth Birthday Jubilee in 1886. As a form of music, it was an important vehicle for expressing Hawaiian royalist sentiments about Hawaiian nationalism during the 1880s and later the overthrow of the monarchy and annexation of Hawai'i by the United States. Because *hula ku'i* was so closely associated with Kalākaua and his supporters, its performance was criticized by antiroyalists.[26] In current practice, *hula* is divided into two major categories: *hula kahiko* ("ancient" *hula),* which is performed to chant and accompanied by traditional instruments; and *hula 'auana* (modern *hula),* which is performed to the accompaniment of Western-influenced melodies and instruments.[27]

New Forms of Hawaiian Music

Hawaiians appropriated Western musical harmonies, forms, and instruments, creating their own styles of contemporary music. The most influential Western form was the Christian hymn (*hīmeni*). One of the first things the missionaries did after they arrived in 1820 was to translate their hymns into Hawaiian and distribute hymnals (words only, at first) throughout the islands. The first hymnal, entitled *Na Hīmeni Hawaii; He Me Ori Ia Iehava, Ke Aukua Mau* (Hawaiian hymns and songs to Jehovah, the Eternal God), was published in 1823 and was extremely popular with the Hawaiians. From 1826 to 1828, forty thousand copies were printed; in 1830, an additional ten thousand copies. Throughout the 1800s, new editions of hymn books in Hawaiian continued to be published; later editions included musical notation as well.[28] As part of their missionary and civilizing activities, the missionaries set up singing schools to teach "good musicianship," which included mastering Western scales and harmony.[29] Hawaiians soon were composing *hīmeni*-like songs, at first simply borrowing Western melodies and giving them Hawaiian lyrics, later composing music and lyrics.[30] Although *hīmeni* was the most influential Western form, the folk tunes of sailors and the secular music of merchants and foreign settlers, popular and classical, were other important influences on Hawaiian music during the nineteenth century.

The most important and influential Hawaiian composers and musicians were the four royal composers: Prince Lileiōhoku, Princess Likelike, King Kalākaua, and Queen Lili'uokalani. Educated at the Chiefs' Children's School by missionary teachers, they learned to play Western musical instruments and throughout their lives were heavily involved in music, Hawaiian and Western, as composers, performers, supporters, and spectators. All knew how to play the piano, guitar, and 'ukulele, and they enjoyed composing music and lyrics and singing with the three royal singing clubs that competed in song contests. Lili'uokalani, the most prolific composer and accomplished musician of the four, composed well over one hundred songs, including "Aloha 'Oe," and directed the Kawaiaha'o Church Choir, also serving as its organist. She was the only Hawaiian composer at the time who could notate her musical compositions, and she was probably the first to have her music published on the mainland, where her songs became popular after the success of "Aloha 'Oe."[31]

In addition to the missionaries, other Westerners played important roles in shaping the new Hawaiian music, most notably the leader of the Royal Hawaiian Band, Henry Berger, whom the German government sent to Hawai'i at King Kamehameha V's request. Berger came in 1872 and led the band until 1915. He also was part of the music program of the Kamehameha Schools and led the Reform School band, the latter becoming his primary source of musicians for the Royal Hawaiian Band. The band played at "boat days" when ships arrived in Honolulu, formal ceremonies, and balls and private parties, where the band became a dance orchestra. In its concerts it played primarily Western classical and band music, but the new Hawaiian song form was also included in its programs (the format of the Royal Hawaiian Band is still much the same). Almost all the musicians in the band were Hawaiian until the overthrow of the monarchy; they resigned en masse rather than sign an oath of allegiance to the new government and play for what was renamed "The Provisional Government Band."[32]

The following famous song, "Kaulana Nā Pua" (Famous Are the Children) was written to protest the annexation and to honor the members of the band for their show of protest:

'A'ole 'a'e kau i ka pūlima
Maluna o ka pepa o ka 'enemi
Ho'ohui 'āina kū'ai hewa
I ka pono sivila a'o ke kanaka.

'A'ole mākou a'e minamina
I ka pu'ukālā a ke aupuni.
Ua lawa mākou i ka pōhaku,
I ka 'ai kamaha'o o ka 'āina.

No one will fix a signature
To the paper of the enemy
With its sin of annexation
And sale of native civil rights.

We do not value
The government's sum of money.
We are satisfied with the stones,
Astonishing food of the land.[33]

By the end of the nineteenth century, Hawaiian songs (often accompanying *hula ku'i*) became the predominant form of symbolic expression. The song form was shaped by Western tonal and chord systems, by Western musical values, by Western views of the individual, and by new instruments, particularly the guitar and *'ukelele*. This form was also shaped by the dynamics of musical performance in a commercial context and new relations between performers and audiences that tended more and more to include Western tourists. Charlot has explored the interaction of Western and Hawaiian forms in his analysis of national anthems written during the monarchy period: "The national anthem is a clear example of an introduced literary form. The model adopted in Hawai'i was *God Save the King*. The poetry is thus in the form of Western lyrics: regular and adapted to Western melody. Moreover, the concepts expressed by that model—most obviously, a Christian theory of kingship—influenced the views expressed in the Hawaiian anthems."[34] The Hawaiianization of the anthem form resulted in a hybrid form that resembled a *mele inoa*, a name chant in praise of a chief.

Similar transformations in the chant form for political campaigns occurred throughout the first three or four decades of the twentieth century as Hawaiians campaigned for elected offices, particularly on the neighbor islands where Hawaiian was still widely spoken. For instance, William Kaho'owaiwai Kāma'u from Hilo ran successfully for the House of Representatives of the Territorial Legislature in 1925 and then for the Senate in 1928. In a 1962 interview he recounted how he campaigned. He credited his victories to his father, who advised him on performing campaign chants: "Your voice is like that of the ocean. Let the voice ride along as the sea, sometimes going up and down, and then crash it against the shore." Kāma'u then chanted for the interviewers one of the chants he had used:

He makamaka no ka ua ia Hilo one
I ka hele no a kipa i Hanakahi.
Kipa aku, ua hala i Makakalo
Ua hele no ā nā 'ale kakali mai.
Ke kakali a'e nei no paha 'oukou ia Kāma'u
Eia au he moho e alualu nei i ka moho senetoa.

The rain is a friend of the sands of Hilo,
And goes a-calling at Hanakahi.
Now that you have called, one is gone to Makakalo,
Has gone where the billows are and there awaits.
Perhaps you are waiting for Kāma'u
Here am I,
A candidate seeking to become Senator.[35]

The new song form did not lend itself to narrative as chant had, for, like most Western forms of music, words became secondary to the music and instrumentation. Nevertheless, throughout the period of the monarchy and into the early territorial period, traditional Hawaiian themes and symbolism were clearly evident in the new songs. In addition to the poetic symbolism, the communal nature of music (e.g., the popularity of glee clubs) and particular uses of the voice were traces of an ancient semantic shaped by Western forms and used for Western purposes, such as political campaigns. Musical performance was one of the few vocational options for Hawaiians, a role that the tourist and recording industries expanded for Hawaiians in the twentieth century. The new Hawaiian song form and modern *hula*, because of their Western content and shape, could be used commercially— cultural novelties that were not so novel that tourists would be bored.

Music and Resistance

Music has been a continuing site of resistance for Hawaiians. Charlot shows how, in successive anthems by Lunalilo, Kalākaua, and Lili'uokalani, increasing stress was placed on chief, land, and people. In *Hawai'i Pono'ī*, composed by Kalākaua, the Christian element has been greatly reduced and traditional Hawaiian views have been emphasized—the chief elevated as the source of well-being and order, the king linked to traditional warrior themes and to Kamehameha I, and the use of traditional honorific terms for a chief. These elements revealed Kalākaua's nationalistic views and his "Hawaii for Hawaiians" theme:

> *Hawai'i Pono'ī* expresses important themes of Kalākaua's thought and policy: a unified nation structured in descending ranks; an activist king in the Kamehameha I tradition; a racial emphasis. . . . Also discreet is the religious but non-Christian character of the anthem. All references to the Christian God are omitted. . . .
>
> As a result, *Hawai'i Pono'ī* seems completely nonreligious and entirely political. The politics of the anthem are, however, Hawaiian: based on traditional views of chiefs that cannot be separated from the indigenous religion. The original title of the anthem, *Hymn of Kamehameha I*, must be taken seriously. *Hawai'i Pono'ī*, like so many postcontact works, seems designed to exploit the gap between Hawaiian

and non-Hawaiian understanding. Such obfuscation is traditionally considered a skill in Polynesian literature and was one which—along with poetic genius and reflection—enabled Kalākaua to create the first truly original Hawaiian anthem.[36]

Resistance in late twentieth-century contemporary Hawaiian music has occasionally been evident in explicitly political lyrics but is found most particularly in the strategic use of the Hawaiian language. Hawaiian words and their hidden meanings—relearned by Hawaiian musicians from *kūpuna (elders), kumu hula,* or in Hawaiian language courses—are used as a way of separating insider from outsider. Words and their meanings have been the only things that Westerners could not totally appropriate, could not buy like they bought land, or remake into their own as they did the political system. Even though wedded to Western forms and the capitalist incentives and constraints of the music market, the continued use of the Hawaiian language in Hawaiian songs is a statement of pride and ethnicity that still inspires the writing of Hawaiian music. Performance of Hawaiian music (ancient, nineteenth and early twentieth centuries, and contemporary) is virtually the only significant public manifestation of a language spoken by few Hawaiians—most of those who speak it well being either elderly Hawaiians, Hawaiian residents of the island of Ni'ihau, or Hawaiian scholars.[37]

Since the 1970s, Hawaiian music has again become a locus of struggle for Hawaiians desiring an authentic presence and self-defined cultural identity. Hawaiian music, as the most public manifestation of Hawaiian culture, continues to carry within its forms and its language the subtext of history, sediments of earlier forms as well as the later forms of the nineteenth and early twentieth centuries, those cultural amalgamations now perceived by many as part of the Hawaiian tradition. Both ancient and not-so-ancient forms of Hawaiian representation are reminders that Hawai'i was once separate, unique, and sovereign. In Hawaiian music there is evidence of what Jameson calls "cultural revolution"—the coexistence of competing sign systems derived from different modes of production—where the old resists assimilation, projecting its own ideological message, calling attention to a history of domination, positioning the dominant culture as *a* culture, not *the* culture, of Hawai'i.[38]

Chapter Six

Transformations in Language and Power

Traditional histories of Hawai'i have largely ignored language, generally treating it as one of many characteristics of culture (on the same level as food, clothing, farming practices, and the like) or as a tool of communication. But if one takes a constitutive view of language—as creative and re-creative, as practical consciousness that saturates and shapes all social activity—then the linguistic intrusion of the West is integral to every aspect of Western penetration and its subsequent domination of the islands.[1] Three fundamental changes in language were initiated in Hawai'i as a result of contact with English-speaking Westerners. Along with the radical shift from orality to literacy came the displacement of Hawaiian by English as the dominant language of discourse. The first altered basic cognitive processes and the second shaped social consciousness. The repositioning of Hawaiians and their culture by Western discourses about Hawai'i further reconstituted social relationships and shifted sites of power. Any one of these linguistic events would have had far-reaching consequences for Hawaiians and their position vis-à-vis Western society; coming together as they did, the effects were compounded.

The Movement from Orality to Literacy

"Writing . . . was and is the most momentous of all human technological inventions. It is not a mere appendage to speech. Because it moves speech from the oral–aural to a new sensory world, that of vision, it transforms speech and thought as well."[2]

In Hawai'i, as in other oral cultures, spoken discourses of social knowledge were integrated into and constitutive of the religious–

political structures and institutions of the islands. It is difficult for those who have internalized the processes and assumptions of writing to understand the thought and social processes of cultures in which words, once spoken, have no residue except for their trace in the human memory. The failure to understand the fundamental differences in human thought processes and modes of communication in oral societies has led to a host of unwarranted assumptions about oral cultures. Oral cultures are usually collapsed by Western or Western-trained observers into "primitive" cultures, always opposed to "advanced" Western cultures in ethnocentric, binary terms: magical versus scientific, wild versus domesticated, closed versus open, concrete versus abstract, prehistoric versus historic, irrational versus rational—terms that carry values associating superiority with the West and that thereby are used to justify domination.

For Westerners, the absence of writing is a characteristic of a primitive culture; poetry or narratives that are not written are dismissed as naive, of interest only to anthropologists but not to Western aestheticians. Consequently, the literate world imposes the condescending terms *oral literatures* or *folk literatures* on the spoken arts of oral cultures and reduces them to predecessors of writing. The word *preliterate,* like the word *prehistory,* carries connotations of unself-consciousness and ignorance—assumptions belied by the poetry and epics produced by skilled oral poets.[3] The fundamental differences in human thought processes and modes of communication between oral and literate societies are not matters of intelligence but of the human brain's cognitive limitations in storing and processing information. Oral cultures have relied on mental techniques and social institutions to store and transmit knowledge that they want to be able to recall, shaping knowledge into forms that lend themselves to memorization, such as lists and structured poetic narratives.

The oral culture of Hawai'i was reflected in the construction of its chanted narratives. Particularly the genealogical and cosmological chants were sources of historical knowledge. Like narratives that could only be expressed orally, Hawaiian cosmological chants were episodic rather than linearly plotted, made up of formulas and standardized themes, peopled with "heavy" characters (the heroic and otherwise memorable), and concretely situated. Their additive, aggregative, and redundant characteristics were related to mental processes of memorization and recall. Words in chants were highly connotative, a communally shared code for referring to histories socially marked as significant. For instance, place names in Hawaiian poetry were embedded with layers of meaning that conjured in the Hawaiian memory and imagination historical events and people, mythical figures and stories associated with those places. To the uninformed, however, chants about places would appear as nothing more than an island travelogue. Martha Beckwith, in her analysis of the *Kumulipo,* speaks of the dominant role of symbolism and *kaona,* the deeper, layered meanings and themes of a chant. Particularly in understanding a long chant, such as the *Kumulipo,* which was composed over many generations, a number of underlying meanings are possible, each plausible in itself for sections of the chant, but difficult to apply to the entire text. "This fitting of images from nature or the habits of daily life into the traditional history of the past, this play of mythical allusion, is what gives value to poetic composition. . . . If the image or allusion can be so turned as to apply to a present situation, so much the better. Back of each image lies an emotional context baffling to the literal translator."[4]

In Hawai'i there was a continuum of linguistic forms and practices from everyday discourse to ritualistic practices. Among the *maka'āinana,* informal storytelling was an interactive process between narrator and audience, drawing on the narrator's memories and knowledge of poems, stories, and histories and the audience's expectations of known myths and tales. But, the production and reproduction of sacred chants (sacred including anything having to do with the gods and the ruling *ali'i*) was central to the structuring of power in Hawai'i. At the highest hierarchical level of the *ali'i,* chant production, transmission, and performance was institutionalized in the *hālau* (schools) and *heiau* (temples) of the priesthoods. The most important chants were entrusted to priests who had been taught the sacred narratives and trained in techniques of memorization and composition and who were then responsible for passing this knowledge on to younger priests.[5] Chants conserved what was socially constituted as relevant, what was worth committing to memory once and recommitting to memory over time—a selective tradition in the strictest sense.

Genealogical chants and lists were mnemonically structured to make it possible to recount an *ali'i's* past ancestors, a requirement for establishing status in Hawai'i. When an individual sought entrance into the inner circle of the reigning *mō'ī*, he was expected to prove his right to be there by reciting his genealogy ten generations back, a feat not just of memory but of social contestation. Malo describes it thus:

> When the king had entered the house and taken his seat,
> in the midst of a large assembly of people including many
> skilled genealogists, two guards were posted outside at the
> gate of the *pa*. . . . When any one presented himself for ad-
> mission to the *hale naua*, or king's house, the guards called
> out "here comes So-and-so about to enter." Thereupon the
> company within called out, "From whom are you descended,
> Mr. So-and-so *naua*? Who was your father, *naua*? To this the
> man made answer, "I am descended from So-and-so; such
> and such a one is my father." The question was then put to
> the man, "Who was your father's father, *naua*? . . . Thus they
> continued to question him until they reached in their inquiry
> the man's tenth ancestor. If the genealogists who were sitting
> with the king recognized a suitable relationship to exist be-
> tween the ancestry of the candidate and that of the king he
> was approved of.[6]

Words, narratives, and rhetoric were endowed with power, not only because they were the sole symbolic and interpretive link with the past, but because they were part of the appropriation, legitimation, and maintenance of power and status by *ali'i* and priests. Some words were heavily endowed with *mana* and therefore *kapu* to those without the status to speak them—to do so meant death. There is a Hawaiian proverb that expresses the power of *'ōlelo* (words). It says, *"I ka 'ōlelo nō ke ola; i ka 'ōlelo nō ka make."*[7] (In the word is life; in the word is death). In Hawai'i, particularly in the context of ritual, words were endowed with power. "Hawaiian tradition holds that a spoken word becomes an actual entity, an operative agent that can bring about events."[8]

Ali'i families had chants that belonged to them as exclusively as the property of things belongs to Westerners. No one outside that genealogical family and its supporting priesthood could perform those chants, for they constituted the legacy of status and power for future generations and ensured the inscription of the current *ali'i* into the ranks of the sacred past. The most important genealogies, or at least the genealogies of *ali'i* in power, were extremely sacred and hence protected and preserved by the priesthoods. For instance, the great cosmological and genealogical chant, the *Kumulipo*, which is 2,102 lines long, was recited by two high-ranking priests only at ceremonies of great political import (perhaps at the *heiau* ceremony in which Captain Cook was received). The chant links the ruling *ali'i* to the primary gods and past diefied chiefs as well as to the stars and all forms of life in the sea and on land. It contains cosmological myths that can be traced back to the Hawaiians' most ancient Polynesian past—even before the Hawaiians themselves came to the islands, when there was only "deep darkness." In the final years of the monarchy, Kalā-kaua, the elected king who was an ancestor of Lono-i-ka-makahiki and who therefore had inherited *the Kumulipo*, had it written down. He modifyed it one final time to legitimate his right to be king and used it to represent the power of the Hawaiian monarchy and defend Hawaiian sovereignty from Western encroachment.[9]

The Power of Writing

By separating the word from living human interaction, by making the word an object on paper or tablet, writing alters communication over time and space. Consciousness is restructured when words are transformed into visual objects that can be stored, consulted, analyzed, compared, and disputed. Writing makes possible complex analytic processes that a purely oral system cannot sustain. Writing does not simply duplicate speech; it changes the nature of language use and opens up different modes of thinking and communication. Writing is necessary for the development of analytical science (but not for knowledge), for historiography (but not for history), for philosophy (but not for religion), for the analysis of symbolic representations themselves—for any processes of highly abstract thought. The *Kumulipo* itself could be subjected to literary analysis only when it had been written down—secured and finally fixed on paper. Even limited literacy can change a previously illiterate individual's orientation to knowledge and reasoning. Although social customs, speech patterns, and narrative practices grounded in orality hold on long past the introduction of writing and printing, patterns of thought and perceptions of what constitutes knowledge change.

It was primarily through the printed word and the mind that the missionaries sought to gain access to the Hawaiian soul.[10] From the accounts of those in early contact with Hawaiians, Hawaiians immediately appreciated the greater power of thought that writing could make possible, and they welcomed the "technologizing" of their language and the printed books of the missionaries, regardless of their content. They reportedly were so keen to learn to read and write that even those reluctant to be Christianized were willing to put up with religious meetings and some of the rules of the missionaries and Ka'ahumanu. Clearly, the missionaries and later the government were successful in teaching Hawaiians to read; by the middle of the 1800s most Hawaiians were literate. At the close of the nineteenth century, 93 percent of Hawaiians and 99 percent of part-Hawaiians over ten years of age were literate, making Hawai'i one of the most literate nations in the world.

But there was a cultural and political price to pay for the achievement of literacy. Literacy, as taught by the missionaries, devalued traditional knowledge, as well as the people who had maintained power through their monopoly of traditional knowledge.[11] Over time, the priests, the chanters, the old people—all those who had been living repositories of knowledge—were displaced as sources of knowledge that mattered in the new material context of the Hawaiians. They were replaced by those willing—indeed determined—to reveal the knowledge contained in books: the written *palapala*. The Reverend John F. Pogue, writing in 1840 and looking back at what the missionaries had accomplished in twenty years, observed the following:

> Twenty years have passed since the Missionaries first came into this garden. . . . Many seeds have been sown. What kind of fruit will be harvested? It is right that we examine the fruits so as to be able to keep in mind the immensity of God's work, and to praise his name. One of the fruits observed consists of the books and the many small tracts that have been published and read from Hawai'i to Kaua'i. The number of pages of printed matter which have been published by the Missionaries from 1820–1840 is about 90,000,000.
>
> The books published are: Holy Bible, complete; New Testament, many printings; Hymn Books, many printings; the Geography of the Religious Tracts; Instructions in Bible Reading; Questions and Answers; History of Hawaii, Gospel History, Ancient History; History of Four-Footed Animals; Spiritual Revelations; Revelations of God. Many small tracts were published for the Sunday schools; the Youth; the Sermons; Readers; Reading and Writing; Geography; Land Transactions, and many more. . . . These books and little tracts have been

read by the people and children by the thousands, and in this way, knowledge and enlightenment have spread throughout these islands.[12]

An article by a C. M. Hyde, identified as being from the North Pacific Missionary Institute (a theological seminary set up by the American Board of Missions in 1877), writing in Thrum's *Annual* for 1891, made the following Foucautian-type observations about the more subtle aspects of the early missionary education processes:

> To be sure, the teaching was of no very high order, boys of fourteen being set to instruct a school, where not only children but parents, and other elderly people as well, came to be taught. The lessons, also, were of no very high grade; reciting Scripture verses in concert, singing a few hymns, in addition to reading, writing, arithmetic, geography. But public school education is a great factor in civilization, accustoming people to act together, to submit to rules, to feel the power of moral principles.[13]

Although Hawaiians continued to pass on their traditional knowledge and cultural practices within the confines of the family and local communities (particularly in areas removed from Honolulu), "the regime of truth" that had resided with the *ali'i* in their compounds and the priests in the *heiau* was subverted by the education offered by the missionaries and encouraged by such *ali'i* leaders as Ka'ahumanu. The long-held assumption that *ali'i* and priests were discursively qualified to exercise power over knowledge—to say "what counts as true"—dissolved in the new cultural order of Hawai'i.[14]

The Displacement of Hawaiian by English

Cultures maintain themselves to the degree by which they maintain their founding symbols and their signifying systems; when language, signifying forms, and discursive practices are lost, community is subverted.[15] Literacy undercut the importance of traditional narratives, devalued oral knowledge, and hence restructured relationships of knowledge and power. The transformation from orality to literacy as occurred in Hawai'i (as in other colonized cultures) also involved violence to the Hawaiian language itself as its sounds, words, and meanings were forced into the symbols, voice, and values of another language. On one level this transformation from one language to another took place in terms of word units and grammar—the substitution of English words for Hawaiian words for objects, practices, states of being, as well as abstract concepts of perception and social valuation. On a deeper level, this process was one in which Westerners, consciously and subconsciously, implanted a new subjectivity, one more hospitable to Christianity and capitalism. It is certainly not irrelevant that those who did the work of transliteration, putting the sounds of Hawaiian into alphabetic symbols of English for the sole purpose of religious and moral instruction, were missionary outsiders working with the haste of those concerned with saving souls.

The shift from orality to writing was accompanied by the social diminishment of Hawaiian and the ascending use and practice of English. With the new language entered a new "will to power": Western values, conceptualizations of truth and reality, and assumptions about Western superiority that were sited in the structure and tropes of English. With English came revaluations and devaluations of Hawaiian practices and knowledge that altered relationships of power between Hawaiians and Westerners. The new language brought other histories and myths of the past, and the Hawaiian past was incorporated into "world" (read *Western*) history as another insignificant strand in the tapestry of "empire" or the "Discovery of the Pacific" or "Manifest Destiny."[16]

With the ascendance of Western material power English became the dominant language. The view that the linguistic domination of English can be explained by the superiority of Western knowledge over that of the Hawaiians assumes that technology and material wealth are evidence of intellectual and even moral superiority. English speakers overpowered Hawai'i by material power; they did so by their control of trade and by their coercive physical power, which, though not often put to use in Hawai'i, could be summoned to enforce a contract or overthrow a government. To use Saussure's words of "chosen" and "tacit convention" to describe the move to dominance of one language over another language is to mystify the multiple elements of power that contributed to the triumph of English.[17]

What then happened as relationships of material power shifted and Hawaiian was replaced by English as the language of knowledge, learning, commerce, and morality? Nietzsche is particularly relevant to understanding the linguistic assault of English on Hawai'i. In his essays on language and power, Nietzsche condemns not so much language in general (although all languages are sites of discursive power) as a particular complex of languages—those informed by a view of Christian morality; more specifically, those shaped by Protestant Christian morality.[18]

What penetrated Hawai'i with English was a particular orientation to morality, human nature, and social relationships. The metaphors, tropes, and logic embedded in English carried new interpretations and representations of reality. With English came new orders of knowledge and new values, and old relations of power dissolved as new ones were constructed. Identities and differences that had been inscribed in Hawaiian were replaced by differences and identities inscribed in English. The very ability to give English names to people, places, and things once heavy with Hawaiian meanings and connotations was an extension of Western control over the islands.[19] It has been advantageous to Westerners to appropriate some Hawaiian words, words like *aloha*, *kuleana*, and *kapu*. But the appropriation has been of sound and sign only; *aloha* has been banalized into the *Aloooooha* of the hotel *lū'au* shows; *kuleana*, which meant the land one cared for and cultivated, has been translated into the English equivalent of "property"; *kapu* has become "keep out," posted on gates to deny access to land that was Hawaiian. Some Hawaiian words and concepts have thus been appropriated and given new metaphorical meanings while being deprived of the "extensive halo" they once possessed in Hawaiian.[20]

For the first four decades or so after contact, English had little impact on the use of the Hawaiian language because trade was carried out primarily in rudimentary Hawaiian or a mixture of Hawaiian and English sufficient for trading purposes. The dominance of Hawaiian began to give way with the arrival of the missionaries, in spite of the missionaries' intention to teach the Hawaiians to read and write in Hawaiian—a quicker way, they felt, of Christianizing them. Within two years after their arrival, as early as 1822, the missionaries, assisted by William Ellis, an English missionary who had been in Tahiti for six years, had fitted Hawaiian orthography into the constraints of only sixteen letters of the English alphabet and were even able to issue a spelling book in Hawaiian. Over the next decades, the missionaries published parts of the Bible (completing the entire Bible in 1839), as well as other teaching materials that included simple histories, natural science texts, and geography texts—all designed to teach the Hawaiians the rudiments of what the missionaries thought any civilized people should know.

At first instruction in English was limited to the chiefs, the chiefs' children, and those who needed English to communicate with Westerners in matters of government and trade. This was the beginning of bilingualism and linguistic dualism (the use of one language for certain activities, the other language limited to other areas). Even though, throughout the period of the monarchy, the official languages of the government were Hawaiian and English, as early as the 1840s laws were being drafted first in English and then translated into Hawaiian. Through the last years of Hawaiian sovereignty, the use of Hawaiian in government gave way to English, English becoming thus the administrative language and the language of power and status.[21]

By the middle of the nineteenth century, language was becoming increasingly problematic for Hawaiians; the logic and concepts of Hawaiian were not consistent with trade and commerce, property as capital, Western social institutions, and new laws of morality that English-speaking missionaries and traders brought to the islands. In the 1850s, there was widespread discussion among Hawaiians, missionaries, and other Western residents on the advantages of Hawaiians learning English. Laws were passed in 1853 and 1854 calling for instruction in English in several island schools; by 1855, ten English schools for Hawaiians were in operation (these were known as "select" schools, distinct from the "common" schools where only Hawaiian was taught; the former charged tuition, the latter were free). The main obstacle to the expansion of English instruction was money and the shortage of English teachers, although the Ministry of Education under Richard Armstrong (1849–1860) advocated the extension of education in English as rapidly as possible.

> Were the means at our command, it would be an unspeakable blessing to have every native child placed in a good English school, and kept there until it had acpuired [sic] a thorough knowledge of what is now, in fact, to a great extent, the business language of the Islands, and which would open to its mind new and exhaustless treasures of moral and intellectual wealth.[22]

The pace of English instruction increased with the passage of the Reciprocity Treaty in 1876 and the great impetus that it gave to the sugar industry. The influx of laborers changed the composition of the schools, and Hawaiian students were soon outnumbered by Asian newcomers for whom the Hawaiian language had no social value. As commerce, conducted primarily in English, intensified in the final decades of the century, occupations off the plantations began to open up for second-generation immigrant children who could speak English. An observer, writing in 1892, one year before the overthrow, observed the following:

While newspapers, weekly and daily, two or three different ones perhaps, are to be found in many Hawaiian families, books of scientific or literary value merely would have but little sale. In fact, there is but a very small profit possible in the sale of books, if a book should be sold to every one of the 8,000 families of Hawaiian speaking people. English must be the language of literature, as it is now the language of business and of courts of law, and of almost every school-room.[23]

English became part of the concrete social and political reality. Increasingly, Hawaiians were forced to engage Westerners in a language whose strategies of discourse and rhetoric were different from those in Hawaiian, and whose metaphors called on a pool of knowledge, mythic and otherwise, unknown to Hawaiians. Hawaiians fighting to preserve the monarchy were forced to debate right and wrong in a language that was inimical to Hawaiian sovereignty. In effect, the struggle was over control of a government already constituted (literally and metaphorically) under a Western godhead, democratic values (albeit not extended to all sectors of the population), and capitalist free enterprise. Physical force, or its threat, removed Hawaiians from the control of the islands in 1893 when Queen Lili'uokalani was deposed from her throne, but language, as much as any other factor, constrained and contained Hawaiian response and action.

After the overthrow of the monarchy, the Americanization of the heterogeneous population became a political as well as a cultural goal of the American political leaders as they consolidated their control over the islands. When the Provisional Government of the Republic banned the use of Hawaiian in government offices, courts, and schools, it was a step that recognized by formal decree what had already been secured in practice. English was inseparable from the material practices of day-to-day life in the urban centers, particularly Honolulu. Hawaiians who did not speak English well withdrew from public arenas, although they continued to debate among themselves in Hawaiian-language newspapers for several decades after the overthrow.[24] Although Hawaiian continued to be the primary language for the majority of Hawaiians throughout the nineteenth century and into the early decades of the twentieth, after English became the prescribed medium of instruction in all schools, each succeeding generation of Hawaiians had less knowledge of and ability to write and speak Hawaiian than the preceding one. As an indication of the rapid ascendance of English after annexation, only 5 percent of Hawaiians over ten years of age could not speak English in 1930, a sizable drop from the 33 percent who could not speak English in 1910.[25]

As the Americanization of Hawaiians became official government policy, language was a cornerstone of acculturating and assimilating Hawaiians and foreign plantation workers. The use of English, whether "proper" English or variants of "pidgin" English, marked and maintained social differences and distinctions well into the twentieth century. How language created types of people is shown in the *Hawaiian Phrase Book*, which was published in 1906 to help English speakers converse with Hawaiians in "the correct colloquial speech of the Hawaiians" and "to teach natives to converse in English." The book is organized topically around various social situations, such as "Conversation with a Native Woman" and "Going to School." In imagined interactions, English speakers are positioned in roles of authority (e.g., the *haole* woman who supervises and trains a native maid in housework and proper attitudes to work and morality or the teacher of ignorant and lazy Hawaiian students), while Hawaiians are placed in roles of servitude or shown as those in need of instruction in Western ways.[26]

Discourses about Chant and *Hula*

During the last years of the eighteenth century and throughout the nineteenth century, Hawaiian chant and *hula* were reconstituted by new discursive formations or, as Foucault prefers to call them, "events"—the emergence of new forces of discursive power.[27] Each of these foreign discourses had its own interpretation and perspective toward chant and *hula*, its particular way of positioning these symbolic practices, of constituting speakers and listeners, and of delimiting the domain of discourse about chant and *hula*. But all were rooted in Western systems of knowledge and Western assumptions about the Other. Nevertheless, just as it is necessary to avoid the ethnocentric bias that the real history of Hawai'i began with Western contact, we must avoid the assumption that discourse about chant and *hula* started with European discoverers or American missionaries.

Hawaiian Discourse about Chant and Hula

There is little written evidence of oral Hawaiian discourse about chant and *hula* prior to Western contact. But with the centrality of chant to Hawaiian society, we can assume that there was an active critical practice. The orality of Hawaiian society meant that the social and communal acts of speaking and listening carried an importance and immediacy far greater than in literate cultures. Although many Hawaiian chants were passed from generation to generation, such as the genealogies and well-known histories of great *ali'i*, often new chants were composed and choreographed for special occasions. Even the genealogical and cosmological chants were altered as sociopolitical relationships changed. Chants, therefore, demanded a "close reading," not only of the connotations of the poetry but of the dance movements of the *hula* choreographed for the chant as well as the total ritual and political context of the performance.[28]

According to Charlot, Hawaiian poets were very attentive to words and meanings and regarded the composition of chants to honor specific *ali'i* on special occasions as opportunities to display "artifice and preciosity" in language.[29] This implies the existence of a group to impress—critics or at least a group of critical peers. In a footnote to Malo's description of the processes involved in composing and performing a *mele inoa* (name chant) to honor a

soon-to-be-born future chief, Nathaniel Emerson, Malo's translator, indicates (in words that impose a literate grid over oral
practices) that a form of critical review was exercised over the
most sacred chants by those responsible for maintaining the oral
traditions. This is not surprising given the power perceived to reside in words and the ideological role of chant in legitimating the
hierarchical social structure.

> When the bards, *peo haku mele,* had composed their *mele,*
> they met at the *ni-o,* a house where were assembled also the
> critics, *poe loi,* the wise men, literati and philosophers, *kak-
> aolelo,* who were themselves poets; and the compositions
> were then recited in the hearing of this learned assembly,
> criticized, corrected and amended, and the authoritative form
> settled.
>
> *Ni-o* (pronounced *nee-o*), and *lo-i* (pronounced *low-ee*) are
> nearly synonymous, meaning to criticize. *Nema* or *nema-
> nema* is to be particular or finicky in criticism.[30]

Emerson's footnote recalls Foucault's discussion of "societies
of discourse" in Greek oral society, where certain individuals
(e.g., the ancient rhapsodists) were responsible for preserving and
producing ritually defined discourses.

> There is no doubt that this division is historically consti-
> tuted. For the Greek poets of the sixth century B.C., the true
> discourse (in the strong and valorized sense of the word), the
> discourse which inspired respect and terror, and to which
> one had to submit because it ruled, was the one pronounced
> by men who spoke as of right and according to the required
> ritual; the discourse which dispensed justice and gave every-
> one his share; the discourse which in prophesying the future
> not only announced what was going to happen but helped to
> make it happen, carrying men's minds along with it and thus
> weaving itself into the fabric of destiny.[31]

The "societies of discourse" in Hawai'i were the most powerful priesthoods (particularly the Kū and Lono priesthoods), those trained in the established poetic traditions, who approved new sacred chants, who upheld the rituals that said who could speak and what could be said, who determined what gestures and signs (i.e., voice quality, instrumentation and style of *hula*) must accompany a particular type of chant, and who knew the efficacy of the words and their effects. "The knowledge in such a society is protected, defended and preserved within a definite group by the often very complex exercises of memory which it implied. To pass an apprenticeship in it allowed one to enter both a group and a secret which the act of recitation showed but did not divulge: the roles of speaker and listener were not interchangeable."[32] Different criteria of excellence and creativity were applied to poets in oral societies. The oral poet worked with formulas, themes, and already-known narratives, recombining and relating them to new contextual situations. The creative work of an individual poet would be absorbed into the compositions of later poets, individual contributions folded into the totality of the chant as it passed from generation to generation.[33]

We can assume that Hawaiian discourse about chant and *hula* was constrained by existing relationships of power and by ideologies of form which are particularly demanding in oral societies. The production and practice of chant and *hula* worked within the a priori rules and categories of the formed tradition, and any chant would be judged on appropriateness of form to content and function, on word use and play, and on individual skill and talent in composing and performing. New chants were judged within the tradition of a given style of chant; if a new chant was found to be aesthetically pleasing and politically appropriate, it was incorporated into the repertoire of chanters, at least for a while. In short, criticism would have been concerned with poetic conventions as well as the aesthetic and artistic qualities of a particular chant.

The total structure of the tradition of chant was always changing as Hawaiian society changed. Since change was structured into Hawaiian society, it follows that its symbolic practices would also have been dynamic. In Hawai'i, however, as in other oral cultures, chant was preserved only in human memory. In such a context, creativity is valued but also suspect; too much tampering threatens the order of the past, the legitimacy of the present, and the ontological security of the future.

Western Discourses about Chant and Hula

The nineteenth-century Western discourses about chant and *hula* objectified them as well as the Hawaiians who performed them. They were inserted into the then-existing Western categories of knowledge about "primitives" and their rites. Hawaiians and their symbolic practices were positioned as objects of spectacle and speculation; only after they had been Christianized and civilized—and therefore "freed" from and outside of their old traditions—were Hawaiians such as Malo, Kepelino, Ī'ī, and Kamakau encouraged by missionaries to write about Hawaiian customs and beliefs.

I have identified three "events" of foreign discourse about chant and *hula:* the discourses of natural history, religion and civilization, and ethnomusicology. Emerging in roughly that order, these discourses were not about the aesthetics of chant and *hula* but about observable behavior and Western interpretations of that behavior: dance movements; dress (or undress); peculiarities of voice and instrumentation; perceived difficences vis-à-vis Western musical practice; and presumed values, functions, and beliefs. Each of these early Western discourses did violence to Hawaiians and their symbolic practices, transposing Hawaiian religion into myth and superstition, worship into pagan rites, sexuality into sin, and poetry into folklore.

Discoverers: The Discourse of Natural History.   In Europe, the eighteenth century was a period of intense curiosity about nature and the distribution of natural species across the continents. The store of knowledge that such explorers as Captain Cook could draw on contrasts sharply with the rude geographical speculations that characterized Columbus's perception of the world in the late fifteenth century: Columbus expected to see mermaids, men with tails, and all kinds of strange human forms; Cook went to fill in the taxonomies of species, to improve navigational technologies, to verify and extend what was already known—his goal, the acquisition of knowledge in the service of trade and commerce. Both Columbus and Cook were seeking wealth: Columbus, gold; Cook, trade.[34] Both offered something in return for the wealth they appropriated: Columbus planned to offer Christianity (the result was enslavement or extermination); Cook planned first to observe and second to civilize and extend British influence.

Cook's voyages of exploration were supreme examples of English research expeditions organized for trade and knowledge in the late eighteenth and early nineteenth centuries. Working within the ideology of colonialization instead of the simpler ideology of fifteenth- and sixteenth-century explorers seeking spice and gold, Cook saw natives as potential subjects capable of producing objects and goods that the British might trade for. Thus, Cook and other British explorers regarded their missions as quite different from those of the early Spaniards. George Dixon, who captained the next mission to Hawai'i after Cook's death, congratulates himself and the other English explorers for elevating "commerce" over the "rapacious desire of accumulating wealth" or the "fame of making discoveries."

There cannot be a greater proof of the truth of this position, than the uniform behaviour of the Spaniards, in the whole course of their almost unbounded acquisitions of discovery, conquest and wealth. The shocking barbarities practised by them when they conquered what was then called the *New World*, cast such an indelible stain on that period of their annals, as *time* can never obliterate.

To the honour of the British Nation be it said, their con-

duct has uniformly been the reverse: whatever unknown
tracts of land they have explored; wherever they found inhabitants, their attention and humanity towards them have
uniformly been such, as to gain the affection, and conciliate
their esteem, instead of exciting their resentment, or incur-
ring their hatred.[35]

Dixon goes on to say that from a commercial point of view, even
the British adventurers of the last century were really little better
than "free-booters," sailing for personal gain rather than for the
benefit of the nation, mankind, navigation, science, and trade—
as were Cook's and his own voyages.

The scientific interest Dixon referred to was the intense interest of Europeans in natural history. In 1735, the Swede Carolus
Linnaeus published his *Systema Naturae*, exemplifying the fas-
cination of Europeans in natural science, specifically in the classification of species. The educated public of Europe delighted in
identifying, classifying, and naming the natural world. Books on
natural history were best-sellers, plants from around the world
were growing in English parks, and animals were collected and
brought back for Europeans to see and wonder about. As Loren
Eiseley notes, "In that time of unfolding beauty the purpose of
science was still largely to name and marvel."[36]

Foucault characterizes this period as one in which natural history was obsessed with the continuity of nature, with the classification of different organisms into orders, classes, genera, and
species—the ordering of "webs of relationships" that were perceived as timeless and fixed. Nature was a table of continuities,
a tightly knit order in the "chain of being" that linked man to
nature. It was a time when observation was privileged, the observable to be captured in language conceptualized unproblematically
as scientific description. The locus of natural history was the
juncture of things and words, between seeing and what one could
say about the seen. The descriptions produced by the gazing observer were meticulous, nontemporal, containing a minimum of

commentary (although certainly more figurative than the positivist scientific language of the next century); they were systematic seeing reduced to the nominative categories of language—seeing only what could be named. "To observe, then, is to be content with seeing—with seeing a few things systematically. With seeing what, in the rather confused wealth of representation, can be analysed, recognized by all, and thus given a name that everyone will be able to understand."[37] Description, thus, was limited to the visible, to surface and lines, to resemblances, affinities, and families. It was naming based on elements of a selected structure; all else was ignored—functions, unseeable tissues and organs, and processes.

In England particularly, the commercial interests of the empire were intertwined with the scientific interests of the era. Captain Cook's three voyages were directly influenced by Linnaeus's work and European interest in the natural wonders of the world. John Ellis, an English collector of specimens, wrote to Linnaeus, describing Cook's preparations for research in these terms.

> No people ever went to sea better fitted for the purpose of Natural History, nor more elegantly. They have got a fine library of Natural History; they have all sorts of machines for catching and preserving insects; all kinds of nets, trawls, drags, and hooks for coral fishing; they have even a curious contrivance of a telescope by which, put into the water, you can see the bottom to a great depth, where it is clear. . . . Besides, there are many people whose sole business it is to attend them for this very purpose. They have two painters and draughtsmen, several volunteers who have a tolerable notion of Natural History. . . . All this is owing to you and your writings.[38]

To the extent that these scientific observers were interested in people, it was as species in the continuum of the natural order. "There was no doubt that the natural science dealt with man as with a species or a genus; the controversy about the problem of races in the eighteenth century testifies to that."[39] Ideas about human cultures were still informed by the old notion of the "chain of being"—a taxonomic ladder on which each species has its place, with humans at the top, just under God, but linked with nature. Within this concept, "man in a state of nature" was little different in his habits from the apes but was capable of progress. Of course, the highest rung of the ladder was occupied by Western man with other races occupying lower rungs, a conceptualization that offered a ready rationalization for imperialism.

Tzvetan Todorov characterizes the study of the Other within this ideological stance as comparative—but limited to comparing Others to Others, not the Other as translatable into Us. Not until the end of the nineteenth century and the epistemic shift that came with ethnography did people and cultures become a separate order of knowledge within the new constraints of the social sciences.[40] Foucault places the emergence of this later ethnographic discourse within a larger epistemic shift affecting language, science, and economy.

> When natural history becomes biology, when the analysis of wealth becomes economics, when, above all, reflection upon language become philology, and Classical *discourse*, in which being and representation found their common locus, is eclipsed, then, in the profound upheaval of such an archaeological mutation, man appears in his ambiguous position as an object of knowledge and a subject that knows.[41]

William Ellis, a surgeon and naturalist on Cook's voyages, demonstrates both the natural history view of man as species in an order of nature and the comparative stance of the Westerner comparing Other to Other. After describing the physical aspects of the islands—how they looked and were situated, the different ecological districts, the soil, the climate, quadrupeds, birds, fish, vegetables, trees, fruits—Ellis moves without pause to the natives, the inhabitants of the habitat, describing their appearance in the same language of descriptive representation: "The men are above the middle size, stout, well made, and fleshy, but not fat. . . . The features of both sexes are good, and we saw some of the females who might really be called fine women." But the language of observation cannot contain the realm of sexuality; there is yet no scientific stance or vocabulary for describing the practices of sex. "There are no people in the world who indulge themselves more in their sensual appetites than these: in fact, they carry it to a most scandalous and shameful degree, and in a manner not proper to be mentioned."[42] Ellis moves to a comparison of dress across the several "specimens" of people that he has observed in his voyage of the Pacific (dress and undress being on the surface and therefore open to the seeing eye and the naturalist's language of representation).

> The poor forlorn inhabitants of Vandieman's land, have as
> little idea of dress as any set of beings in the world. . . . The
> new Zealanders have a greater claim to taste. The men wear
> a ha-hoo over their shoulders. . . . The refined natives of the
> Friendly Isles are very careful in their dress. . . . At Otaheitee
> and the Society Isles, the dress of both sexes is nearly the
> same. . . . The continent of America affords a striking contrast
> to the last two mentioned people . . . here filth and dirt seem
> to be the principle objects.

Ellis's comparative perspective of noting differences and similarities among several cultures is also evident in his description of chant and *hula*. The Hawaiians' "music" is likened to that of the Tahitians, the Eskimos, and the Indians.

> Their songs are not various; they are sung nearly in the same
> tone as at Otaheitee, but their dances are different from any
> we have yet seen. They have none of those graceful move-
> ments which are so peculiar to the natives of Anamooka,
> Amsterdam, etc. nor the lewd motions which characterize the
> people of the Society Isles. Whenever they can collect seven
> or eight girls together, they generally strike up a dance, which

is an amusement they are very partial to. They first begin by repeating, or rather singing several words which appear to be in rhyme, all of them at the same time slowly moving their legs and striking their breasts gently with their right hands; this being finished, they all jump in a violent manner, but in exact time, striking their breasts or sides much harder than before, and repeating the word he'ora; those who continue this exercise the longest, are allowed to be the best dancers. This, with very little variation was the only dance we saw, except one, which was performed by an old woman, and accompanied with a drum. The movements were something like those of our hornpipes; she had bracelets composed of dog's teeth, fixed upon a kind of netting, round her ancles [*sic*], which by the continual motion her legs were in, made no disagreeable music. The drum was beat by a man, who at the same time accompanied it with a song.[43]

Descriptions of what these voyagers saw were not limited to words. Artists also went on the voyages of Cook and other explorers of the Pacific. They were as limited in their representations by the classical conventions of seeing and art as the scientific observers were by the natural science conventions of knowing and describing. European artists painted Pacific islanders in the classical style of the time, draping Polynesians in togas resembling those of the ancient Greeks. It was difficult for them to capture the light and intense colors of the Pacific or represent the gestures, posture, and physiognomy of islanders.[44]

After the departure of Cook's two ships in February 1779 (with what little remained of Cook), it was not until 1786 that the next foreign ships visited Hawai'i. George Dixon, the commander of one of the British ships that came that year and returned again the next, was maybe the first to apply the notion of "lack" to Hawaiian music in comparison to Western music; lack of harmony, lack of scale, lack of instrumentation. The concept of lack was a recurring theme in discourses about Hawaiian music throughout the nineteenth century. Dixon's sensitivity to the poetic nature of chant—"I had almost said poetry"—and his allusions to contemporary topics as sources of amusement are unusual among early (and even many later) observers. Dixon anticipates the shift from comparative (Other to Other) to the more relativistic stance of the later nineteenth century (comparing Other to Us).

The heevas, or songs, cannot be described by notes, as they rather resemble a quick energetic manner of speaking, than singing; and the performers seem to pay more attention to the motions of the body than the modulations of the voice. The women are the most frequent performers in this kind of merriment; they begin their performance slow and regular, but by degrees it grows brisker and more animated, 'till it terminates in convulsions of laughter. It is very evident that these people have not the least idea of melody, as the tones and modulation in all their songs are invariably the same; however, there seems to be some degree of invention (I had almost said poetry) in the composition of the words, which are often on temporary subjects; and the frequent peals of laughter are no doubt excited by some witty allusion or other contained in them.[45]

Within a few years after Dixon's 1786 visit, Hawai'i had become a regular port of call for trading vessels and ships of various foreign navies. Captain George Vancouver visited Hawai'i five times, twice with Cook (1778 and 1779) and three times as commander of an exploring expedition (1792, 1793, and 1794). Impressed with the obvious value of the islands, he tried, by developing a friendly and helpful relationship with Kamehameha I, to attach the islands to the British Empire.[46] During his visits, Vancouver observed several performances of chant and *hula*. On one visit, he spent several days with Kamehameha on the island of Hawai'i, during which there were several "pleasant" evenings of singing and dancing. One occasion was particularly "splendid," in which "ladies of consequence" who were attendants of Kamehameha performed to honor a princess, although she was not present at the event.

In his lengthy description, Vancouver makes use of Western theatrical metaphors. There had been many "rehearsals" for this performance, which took place in a "theatre," a site chosen for the accommodation of the more than four thousand "spectators." Everyone in attendance was dressed in their best apparel, including clothes for which they had bartered with Vancouver. They were so elaborately adorned that they "presented a very gay and lively spectacle," constituting for Vancouver a double spectacle: the performance of the chant and *hula* positioned within the larger spectacle of Hawaiians, the latter being the principal object of Vancouver's gaze.

Having arrived early, Vancouver was escorted to the "green room" where the "actresses" were preparing themselves, asking Kamehameha, who was also present and "who was considered to be a profound critic," for his directions in the arrangement of their dress. When they were finally ready, the "conductor of the ceremonies, and sole manager" of the occasion made an apology to the "audience" that produced a laugh. He then caused the "music" to begin. The "band," consisting of five men, chanted first and then the actresses took their place. The "heroine" of the piece was one of seven actresses, all identified by Vancouver as *ali'i* women, including the captive daughter of Kahekili, the great Maui chief.

> This representation, like that before attempted to be described, was a compound of speaking and singing; the subject of which was enforced by appropriate gestures and actions. The piece was in honor of a captive princess, whose name was Crycowculleneaow; and on her name being pronounced, every one present, men as well as women, who wore any ornaments above their waist, were obliged to take them off, though the captive lady was at least sixty miles distant. This mark of respect was unobserved by the actresses whilst

engaged in the performance; but the instant any one sat down, or at the close of the act, they were obliged to comply with this mysterious ceremony.

The variety of attitudes into which these women threw themselves, with the rapidity of their action, resembled no amusement in any other part of the world within my knowledge, by a comparison with which I might be enabled to convey some idea of the stage effect this produced, particularly in the three first parts. . . . In each of these first parts the songs, attitudes, and actions, appeared to me of greater variety than I had before noticed amongst the people of the great South Sea nation, on any former occasion.[47]

Unfortunately, at least in Vancouver's mind, the fourth part or "act" departed drastically from the first three. Probably a *hula ma'i* (a *hula* praising the genitals and procreative power of an *ali'i*), this dance was outside the pale of decency even for Vancouver, who seems throughout his journals to have made a point of representing Kamehameha and the Hawaiians as favorably as possible. As with William Ellis on Cook's voyages, no socially acceptable words could describe the sexual content and motions of the *hula ma'i*.

Had the performance finished with the third act, we should have retired from their theatre with a much higher idea of the moral tendency of their drama, than was conveyed by the offensive, libidinous scene, exhibited by the ladies in the concluding part. The language of the song, no doubt, corresponded with the obscenity of their actions; which were carried to a degree of extravagance that was calculated to produce nothing but disgust even in the most licentious.[48]

But obviously only Vancouver was disgusted, for the Hawaiians left "in the greatest good humour; apparently highly delighted with the entertainment they had received." Immediately following this theatrical spectacle, it then being dark, Vancouver returned the hospitality and entertainments offered by the Hawaiians with a show of fireworks that, as an earlier entry in his journal makes clear, was calculated to both amuse and impress the Hawaiians, "to impress the minds of these people more deeply with our superiority."[49]

Of the early observers of Hawaiian chant and *hula*, none was more enthusiastic than Adelbert von Chamisso, an artist who sailed as a naturalist on the Russian expedition under the command of Otto von Kotzebue in 1816. By that time, the islands were already engaged in considerable trade, particularly in sandalwood, which was still under Kamehameha's control. Chamisso seems to have had a better understanding than most Western observers of Hawaiian religion, law, and social practices. He is more distinctly relativistic than Dixon in drawing analogies between Hawaiians and Europeans, noting similarities between Hawaiian religion and Christianity and Hawaiian customs of hospitality with Russian customs. Chamisso speaks of the Hawaiian "liturgy and . . . holy practices," comparing them to his own religious practices: "As in the Catholic liturgy, the people join in here and there in the chanting of the officiating priest."[50] Chamisso's greater sensitivity than that shown by other observers of Hawaiian culture can be seen in his notes about their sexuality and what he perceives as its perversion by Westerners: "To this people, I maintain, that chastity as a virtue was foreign: we have inoculated it with covetousness and greed and stripped it of modesty."[51]

Chamisso is unique in placing chant and *hula* in the realm of the aesthetic, recognizing the close relationship between poetry, music, and dancing, which "appear hand in hand, in their original union." In an ecstatic description of the "hurra-hurra," Chamisso again makes a connection between Hawaiian culture and his own.

Truly, since I have often seen the ungraceful contortions that we admire in our dances under the name of ballet, it seems to me after observing and viewing the magnificence of the local performances that the former pale in comparison. We barbarians, we call the natives who have a love of the beautiful "savages," and we have allowed the ballet of the confounded poets and of the mournful mimics to drive them out of the halls we boast are devoted to art. . . . I must give you an indication that I am not exaggerating. On the 4th of December three men danced, and on the 6th, a large group of young girls, amongst whom were many of exceeding beauty. . . . One may glance at the two horrible drawings which spoil Choris' atlas. The dance does not lend itself to being painted, and for what he has here done, may the Genius of Art forgive him.[52]

Chamisso stands in the gap between the early comparativist natural history discourse, which sought to name and classify unknown human species into an order of identity and difference, and the later relativist discourses of ethnography and ethnomusicology, which in their embryonic stages were concerned with the organic structure of cultures and the functions of their practices.

The Missionaries: The Discourse of Religion and Civilization. The discourses of Christianity and natural history overlapped. They shared assumptions of a Divine Order, a Chain of Being, and a hierarchical relationship between the West and the rest of the world. But the discourses were radically different in their views of human nature: to the missionary mind, the natural disposition of man or woman was to indulge in "sordid, selfish, sinful passions."[53] Instead of the naturalist's more dispassionate description and classification, that of the removed and passing observer, the missionaries were intensely involved. They were engaged in spreading the Word of God and struggling with evil in order to save heathen souls. Hiram Bingham, leader of the first company of missionaries, starts his account of his mission to Hawai'i with these words: "Darkness covered the earth and gross darkness the people. This, for ages, was emphatically applicable to the isles of the great Pacific Ocean. But the voice divine said, 'Let there be light.' "[54] The mission of saving souls was inseparable from civilizing the body and teaching the mind. The missionaries were instructed by the American Board of Missions to acquaint "so rude, so dark, so vile a part of the world," with the "way of life"; this included not only teaching Hawaiians about Christianity and salvation but "everything in the way of civilization": "to fill the habitable parts of those important islands with schools and churches, fruitful fields, and pleasant dwellings."[55]

The American missionaries came from New England, a part of the country shaped by the struggles of Puritan Protestantism against European Catholicism and kingly authority. It was a society that had as part of its immediate past (and the myths already constructed of that past) a history of "civilizing the savage," a process that in the early 1800s was still far from complete as Americans continued to push westward toward the Pacific. Even as the Mission Board was making preparations to send missionaries to Hawai'i, it was concerned with the continuing process of civilizing American Indians, of overcoming their "intransigence" and resistance to Western economy, government, labor, language, and religion.[56] For Hawai'i and the Hawaiians, this meant that the New England missionaries came not only with a gospel but armored with already-formed expectations of what the uncivilized were like. There was none of Rousseau's "noble savage" in missionary conceptions of the Pacific islanders, only "children of evil and of outer darkness."[57]

The British missionary William Ellis, who had spent several years in Tahiti before he came to assist the American missionaries in 1822, distinguished between Captain Cook's romanticized descriptions of the Hawaiians and the "truth" as perceived by the missionaries.

> The descriptions which Captain Cook's Voyages contained, of the almost primitive simplicity, natural vivacity, and fascinating manners, of a people, who had existed for ages, isolated, and unknown to the rest of the world, were so . . . enchanting, that many individuals were led to imagine they were a sort of elysium, where the highly favoured inhabitants . . . dwelt

in what they called a state of nature, and spent their lives in unrestrained enjoyment. . . . Far different are the impressions produced on the minds of the Missionaries who have resided for some years in the islands. Having acquired their language, observed their domestic economy, and become acquainted with the nature of their government, the sanguinary charac-ter of their frequent wars, their absurd and oppressive system of idolatry, and the prevalence of human sacrifices, they are led . . . to more just and accurate conclusions—conclusions in awful accordance with the testimony of divine revelation.[58]

Not only were the American missionaries products of their rigid Protestant upbringing, but they had been influenced by an evangelical movement that was sweeping New England. In the early nineteenth century, the northeastern seaboard of the United States was undergoing the first stages of industrialization and eco-nomic expansion. Powerful merchant families were establishing themselves, much of their fortunes derived from trade oriented to the Pacific and therefore involving Hawai'i. This capitalist expan-sion of the United States, the growing secularization of American society, and the increasing ethnic and religious heterogeneity of New England were sharpening class distinctions with parallel divisions among various religious sects and congregations. The growth of Catholicism with increasing numbers of Catholic im-migrants from Ireland and other Catholic countries was particu-larly hard for some New England Protestants to accept.

During the early 1800s, an evangelical religious movement vari-ously referred to as the New Divinity Movement and the "Second Great Awakening" developed in response to the social changes taking place. This religious movement was an extreme form of Calvinism, one that demanded of its adherents protestations of personal conversion, constant striving for salvation, and zealous commitment to work for God's kingdom.[59] Linked to the mis-sionary impulse of this religious movement was an element of national pride that came out of the not-too-distant experience of achieving national sovereignty, as well as the successful conclusion of the War of 1812, during which the United States won several key victories that increased its territory. This nationalism was reflected in the missionaries' interest in bringing not just Western civilization to Hawai'i but the American version of it. It combined the impulse to accumulation with a frugal lifestyle and a distinct moral outlook that projected religious behavior into the day-to-day world. Clearly, the missionaries were a major factor in the increasing domination of Hawai'i by the United States throughout the nineteenth century. The missionaries that came to Hawai'i were inspired by the language and theology of evangelism and the nationalist pride of a country "on the move." They were people willing, even determined, to sacrifice the comforts of life, even life itself, to fulfill what they defined as a divine mission.

The rigidity of the early missionaries' Calvinist doctrine was evident in their limiting church membership only to those who had a true conversion experience, which included adopting Western ways. When Ka'ahumanu, the powerful regent, wanted to be baptized in 1824, Bingham was reluctant: "We dared not authorize such a step till we had more decisive evidence that she had been born from above by the power of the Spirit of God." Not until December 1825, five years after the missionaries arrived, were a small number of Hawaiians, all *ali'i* and including Ka'ahumanu, taken into the church.[60] During the first seventeen years of the mission, only thirteen hundred Hawaiians were allowed to join because the missionaries were not convinced that the Hawaiians had really undergone a total spiritual and social transformation. Finally, at the prodding of the Board of Missions back home, the "great revival" took place; from 1837 to 1840 nearly twenty thousand Hawaiians were baptized. By 1840, Hawai'i was officially a Christian nation, or at least it was decreed so in the constitution: "That no law shall be enacted which is at variance with the word of the Lord Jehovah, or at variance with the general spirit of His word. All laws of the islands shall be in consistency with the general spirit of God's law."[61] Not all the missionaries shared the extreme ascetic orientation of Bingham, who perceived any deviance from his own moral values as sinful.[62] Those who came in the capacity of printers, farmers, and teachers, and the later companies of missionaries, tended to be more tolerant of Hawaiian cultural practices.

Despite the missionaries' attempt to stay out of business and government, their religious goals were inseparable from capitalism and American hegemony. As Hawaiian leaders recognized that they needed to be more knowledgeable about the West if they were to hold their own in trade and politics, they asked the missionaries to teach them about the world, including the principles of Western economy. William Richards, a missionary, was hired by the *ali'i* in 1838 to teach them about law, political economy, and the science of government. Lecturing in Hawaiian, Richards used Francis Wayland's *Elements of Political Economy,* a text published in 1837: "In these illustrations I endeavored as much as possible to draw their minds to the defects in the Hawaiian practices, and often contrasted them with the government and practices of enlightened nations. . . . When the faults of the present system were pointed out & the chiefs felt them & then [they] pressed me with the question, Pehea la e pono ai, [How shall we be pono]?"[63]

Missionaries and the Hula.   The missionaries were preoccupied with virtue and morality—their own as well as that of the Hawaiians. Their liturgy reflected their denial of self, particularly the sexual self and sensual pleasure; for them, passion must always be subordinate to reason.[64] The sermon, prayer, and hymn were the central parts of the Protestant ritual, with the written word, the Bible, the final symbol of authority.[65] There was little of the sensual visible world, and the "idolatry" of the Hawaiians (as well as that of the persecuted Catholics) was an abomination to these Puritan iconoclasts. It is not hard to imagine, and their words make it clear, how shocked and horrified the missionaries were by the Hawaiians' religious practices and particularly their state of undress and liberal sexuality. While some of the European explorers were romantics who associated nakedness with untainted innocence, ascetic Calvinist missionaries saw it as a sign of libidinous behavior, depravity, and a lack of civilization. Missionary women, in particular, were determined to get Hawaiian women to clothe themselves in long dresses (*mu'umu'u*) and with bonnets and shoes.[66]

In the missionaries' constant drive to substitute piety for sexuality, nothing upset them more than the *hula;* it was sin in its most open manifestation. Throughout the years of the mission, *hula* was increasingly constrained, first by clothing the dancers and banning the dance on the Sabbath, and later by prohibiting its performance, at least around areas where missionaries and converted chiefs resided. Not until later Hawaiian monarchs challenged "mission rule" was *hula* celebrated in public performance.

The missionary discourse directed against chant and *hula* stripped away religious meaning, converting beliefs into mere "superstition" while focusing on manifestations of "heathenistic" practices, "idolatrous" behavior, and explicit sexuality. Bingham described a dance that occurred in the second year of the mission, as Hawaiians in Honolulu prepared for the return of Liholiho (Kamehameha II) from Kailua by practicing their "heathen song and dance." For many weeks, "the first sound that fell on the ear in the morning was the loud beating of the drum. . . . Day after day, several hours in the day, the noisy hula" went on next to the house of the governor. Except for decorations of *kapa* (cloth made of bark), leaves, flowers, and dogs' teeth around the ankles, "much of the person is uncovered; and the decent covering of a foreign dress was not then permitted to the public dancers." Bingham described the formation and motions of the dancers, the instruments, the notes and tempo of the chants, noting the extreme exertions of the sweaty dancers and concluding that "the whole arrangement and process of their old hulas were designed to promote lasciviousness." He observes that "Liholiho was fond of witnessing them, and they were managed to gratify his pride and promote his pleasure."[67] Although the missionaries tried to get Liholiho to suspend the daily dancing, at least on Sundays, the king replied, "This is the Hawaiian custom, and must not be hindered." When pressed again, Liholiho again refused: "I wish to see them dance to-day." When the king finally agreed to suspend dance the following Sunday, Boki, the governor of Oʻahu and a consistent opponent of the missionaries, said "with magisterial and atheistic air, 'dance we will—no tabu.' " When Bingham again approached the king and queen about the "idolatry and licentiousness" of *hula*, they assured him that it was " 'play, and not idol worship.' "[68]

Until the overthrow in 1893, the performance of chant and *hula* was an arena of struggle between Western domination and Hawaiian resistance. The early resistance of Liholiho was followed by the rebelliousness of his successor, Kauikeaouli (Kamehameha III), against the puritanical demands of Kaʻahumanu and Kinaʻu, the strong female regents who were enthusiastic Christian converts. For the last two Kamehameha kings (Alexander Liholiho and Lot Kamehameha), and particularly for the elected king, Kalākaua and his sister, Queen Liliʻuokalani, chant and *hula* were enjoyable entertainments, but more important, they were symbols of Hawaiian sovereignty.

There were three major transformations in the meanings of chant and *hula* in the nineteenth century. The first occurred when Liholiho and his *aliʻi* abolished the *kapu* system in 1819, one year before the missionaries arrived. This undercut the traditional religious–political significance of chant and *hula*, but did not detract from their aesthetic, cultural, and entertainment values. The second transformation in meaning came with the discourse and actions of the missionaries that inserted guilt and shame into the performance of chant and *hula*. The third was the explicitly political significance given chant and *hula* by Hawaiian nationalists, who used them to symbolize Hawaiian power before Western penetration and mobilize Hawaiian resistance to further Western encroachments after the mid-1850s.

With the formal end of the mission in 1864, the most vituperative criticisms of chant and *hula* abated, but the moral discourse continued into Kalākaua's reign (1874–1891). His encouragement of chant and *hula* at 'Iolani Palace was used by his critics as evidence of his intransigence and proof of his unfitness to rule—they derisively called him the "Merrie Monarch," now used as a term of respect and affection by Hawaiians to acknowledge his revival of, and contributions to, chant and *hula*. By that time, however, the discourse of theology had been replaced by a discourse of economy and a new discourse of culture. Even those still concerned about public morality were less concerned with Christianizing than with Americanizing what was rapidly becoming an ethnically diverse island society. This preoccupation with Americanizing the islands was part of a larger national movement to fashion a common integrative culture based on middle-class definitions of taste and refinement, a politics of culture that took place throughout the United States after the Civil War.[69] Within the new discourse of culture, *hula* was no longer "evil" (particularly now that Hawaiians were dressed and the most explicitly sexual dances removed from their repertory); instead, *hula* was seen as pleasant and harmless entertainment and a possible cultural commodity that could be economically exploited to attract and amuse the growing number of visitors to Hawai'i.

The Musicologists: The Discourse of Science.   Western musicological discourse about chant and *hula* emerged in the latter half of the nineteenth century. It focused on the components, elements, and structure of the "music" itself, imposing Western knowledge about music on Hawaiian oral practices. It was concerned with analyzing the sound and structure of Hawaiian chant as music, not as poetry and meaning.

Musicology as a field of knowledge developed first in German-speaking countries, where the study of music turned from philosophical contemplation of music and its aesthetics to what the Germans called *musikwissenschaft*. Whereas previously Europeans interested in music had studied it as part of Western social history, musicology focused attention on two relatively narrow areas of study: the high-art tradition of Western music, its archives, and its history; and music theory, the analysis of the technical aspects of the structure of music, including scales, chords, time, and so on—"those aspects of music that might be thought analogous to vocabulary, grammar, syntax, and rhetoric in the field of language."[70]

As musicology became established as an academic discipline, it excluded the meaning, aesthetics, emotions, and social function of music (the latter aspect was recovered in a particular way by ethnomusicology in the next century). As a form of positivism applied to music, musicology became obsessed with the feasibility of representing sound and the structured sound of music— questions of what makes a piece of music "work"—in language, attempts that never fully succeeded.[71] As a field of study, musicology met Foucault's definition of a discipline as a principle of limitation that gives the impression of infinite resources for creating knowledge while actually restricting and constraining what can be studied and said. "A discipline is defined by a domain of objects, a set of methods, a corpus of propositions considered to be true, a play of rules and definitions, of techniques and instruments. . . . Within its own limits, each discipline recognizes true and false propositions; but it pushes back a whole teratology of knowledge beyond its margins."[72]

Although *ethnomusicology* (the applications of musicology to the "music" of non-Westerners) did not develop as an academic field until the 1950s, there was within the early formation of musicology an interest in European folk music and non-Western music that was generally referred to as "comparative musicology."[73] The European interest in folksongs (and later the music of other cultures) fit the same conventions and limitations of knowledge that Foucault identified with the classifying impulse of natural history. But instead of mapping differences and similarities across species, musicologists mapped music across cultures, applying Western categories of classical and primitive, structurally comparing various cultures' music in terms of tones, intervals, scales, and the like, with Western classical forms used as the benchmark of comparison.

Although the first systematic, comparative study of Hawaiian music was not done until Helen Roberts, one of the first American ethnomusicologists, studied chant in the 1920s, technical descriptions of Hawaiian chant were attempted in the last decades of the 1800s.[74] In Thrum's *Hawaiian Almanac and Annual for 1886*, A. Marques (cited as a "foreigner who has made a prolonged stay in this country") writes about Hawaiian chant, first noting the difficulty of doing so because civilization had made a "clean sweep of their old customs"—the older Hawaiians having died off and the younger ones ignorant of the old ways. In his analysis, Marques compares Hawaiian music to songs and dances he had seen or heard in Africa, the Middle East, Tahiti, other island cultures, as well as to Western music. In his comparisons with the latter, the dominant theme is the "lack" of complexity of Hawaiian music.

> The ancient Hawaiians knew of nothing similar to our modern music, with its regular intervals, its progressive scales, either natural or chromatic, and its varied modulations. . . .
> But now is the place to remark that all the other Hawaiian instruments, both wind and string, were constructed for giving only two or at the utmost three notes. . . . It can thus be safely inferred how primitive must have been the old Hawaiian idea of music.[75]

Marques then offers a detailed analysis of the structure of the "music" in terms of what it has—or more notably does not have—in terms of notes and tones (tonic, dominant, subdominant, inferior, etc.), chords, singing in unison or parts, harmony, fifths (consecutive or forbidden), time (2-4,4-4,3-4,6-8), and so on. Throughout this description is the explicit and implicit assumption of Western superiority in music. For instance, Marques remarks about the trouble Mr. Berger, leader of the Royal Hawaiian Band, has in training "natives" and "band boys" to keep good time in waltz pieces. "That these difficulties of time can however be overcome, is shown by the immense repertory of difficult operatic music so well played by the Royal Hawaiian Band, which under the leadership of one foreigner, is composed exclusively of natives."[76]

Marques concludes by describing the "modern state of art" in Hawaiian music, crediting the missionaries and Berger with improving the "taste and faculties of the natives for music"—how "ludicrously" the "barbarians" sang at first, before they could overcome their "chanting routine." Yet, Marques notes, the "native progress in music" has been considerable over the past twenty years, Hawaiians even composing their own "simple, graceful and effective," if unoriginal, compositions. "Yet they do not assimilate readily all kinds of European music," nor do they take "readily to our instruments," with the exception of the guitar and *'ukulele*. Marques concludes with observing "the wonderfully improved dispositions of the natives" and says he hopes that someday Honolulu will have a regular conservatory of music.[77] More than twenty-five years later, Marques still writes of the Hawaiians' "deficiences," but he rather grudgingly concedes that in spite of all these drawbacks and of this "childish immaturity, the amateur and enthusiast finds himself charmed and held as in the clutch of some Old World spell, and this at what others will call the dreary and monotonous intoning of the savage."[78]

Of the three nineteenth- and early twentieth-century discourses about Hawaiian chant and *hula*, that of musicology was the most objectifying. It became even more so as "comparative musicology" left the hands of amateurs like Marques and moved into the disciplinary boundaries of ethnomusicologists, who combined the technical discourse of music with the new social science discourse of anthropology. Modern ethnomusicology's conventions of scientific objectivity obscure the subjective valuations that were so obvious in the descriptions of Marques. Instead, the ethnomusicologist now speaks as the expert (university certified, not an amateur), primarily addressing other experts who share a specialized language that deconstructs chant into tones, intervals, tempo, and the like (the music itself), and into ritual, custom, and function (the music in culture). It is behavior (as performance) and sounds (as vocalizing or instrumentation), as they can be captured in written–notational forms, that interest most ethnomusicologists, at least within the confines of their discipline.[79] It is mainly in their attempts to devise descriptive notations that can represent all sounds, and distinctions among sounds, that the positivistic dichotomy between subject and object is most apparent. In fact, it is in efforts to avoid Western bias (to come up with systems of transcribing music outside Western notation), that the music as an object for dissection is most apparent.[80] Because of its essentialist discourse and its concern to preserve cultural forms of expression that are in danger of disappearing, ethnomusicology has tended to marginalize forms of music that combine imported and indigenous contemporary musics, such as the *hapa-haole* music of the 1930s that combined Tin Pan Alley and Hawaiian music and more contemporary popular music, such as the "Jawaiian" music of the 1990s that combines Jamaican reggae and Hawaiian contemporary music.

Since the 1970s, the study of Hawaiian music has been brought into the cultural politics of the Hawaiian renaissance. As the production and performance of chant and *hula* have been politicized by Hawaiian musicians and scholars, it is no longer possible to ignore the meanings of Hawaiian music—past or present. Ethnomusicologists such as Adrienne Kaeppler and Elizabeth Tatar now focus on the interaction of history, form, and aesthetics in their analyses of the complex styles and forms of chant and *hula,* old and new, as well as newer forms of Hawaiian music.

Conclusion

The three nineteenth-century Western discourses constructed different definitions of Hawaiians and their chant and *hula.* All three privileged foreign speakers—explorers–natural scientists, missionaries, musicologists—over Hawaiians. The myths generated by each of these foreign discursive regimes now constitute much of the received understanding of ancient practices of Hawaiian chant and *hula* and the larger, blurred genres of Hawaiian music since the nineteenth century. In *Orientalism* Edward Said analyzes the imposition of Western categories on other histories and cultures.

This whole didactic process is neither difficult to understand nor difficult to explain. One ought again to remember that all cultures impose corrections upon raw reality, changing it from free-floating object into units of knowledge. The problem is not that conversion takes place. It is perfectly natural for the human mind to resist the assault on it of untreated strangeness: therefore cultures have always been inclined to impose complete transformations on other cultures, receiving these other cultures not as they are but as, for the benefit of the receiver, they ought to be.[81]

The creation of a new social structure for the islands, whether intended or not, resulted in loss of life, land, language, and power for the Hawaiians. Whether it also meant the loss of Hawaiian "culture" is a matter that is intensely debated in the present.

Chapter Seven

Contending Representations of Hawaiian Culture

For more than twenty-five years, during the spring in the city of Hilo on the Big Island, practitioners and lovers of Hawaiian chant and *hula* have gathered for the Merrie Monarch Festival. The three-day event holds great emotional and cultural significance for many Hawaiians, uniting performers and audience in the celebration of *hula*. That *hula* is a symbol of Hawaiian pride and identity is as evident in the controversies that erupt from time to time over the interpretations of ancient chants and *hula* as it is in the execution of the dances. For many Hawaiians, but particularly for the participating *hālau*, the festival is the high point of the year, the climax of year-long efforts of preparation, practice, and fund raising by the *kumu hula*, their students, friends, and families.

Competition has become an important part of the practice of *hula* in Hawai'i.[1] In addition to the Merrie Monarch Festival, the annual King Kamehameha Hula and Chant Competition started in 1973 is a major event. Like its better-known counterpart on the Big Island, it has competition in both *hula kahiko* (ancient styles) and *hula 'auana* (modern styles). In 1987, more than thirty dance performances were performed in male, female, and combined categories within the two styles of *hula*. In addition, more than ten chanters competed. The annual Prince Lot Hula Festival on O'ahu is the third major annual event for *hula* and chant. In addition to these, numerous other performances take place during the course of a year where *hula* is featured, primarily for local audiences.

While the spirit of competition often overshadows devotion to tradition, in the 1986 Merrie Monarch, culture took precedence over competition. Just as the festival started, an unusually violent storm began, the heavy rains ending a long period of drought for the island. The fury of the storm mounted during the second night of the *hula kahiko* competition, plunging the arena into darkness for more than forty minutes; when power was restored, Māpuana de Silva, the *kumu hula* of the next-to-perform *hālau* (one of the strongest contending groups) announced that her dancers would not dance. "Hālau Mōhala 'Ilima will not be performing here tonight. We feel it is not appropriate for us to perform. My first concern is for my dancers and caring for them. Thank you." As a spokesman for the group explained later, the women of the *hālau* had interpreted the storm as a sign that they should not dance the Moloka'i chant of the Goddess Hina, that to do so might bring on Hina's final destructive storm. Another *kumu hula* almost withdrew. "My first thought was I was going to pull my girls. . . . I really believe Hina was here last night. She came to watch and be part of this whole festival." But this *kumu hula* changed his mind because he also believes in the Christian God: "All of a sudden I had a nice, warm feeling." The next day, the press quoted various *kumu hula* and *kūpuna* (elders) as to their reactions to the storm and to Hālau Mōhala 'Ilima's withdrawal. Opinion was split between those who believed the storm to be a sign of displeasure from the Hawaiian Goddess Hina and those who saw it as a drought-ending blessing from the Christian God.[2] This episode reveals the ambivalence of many Hawaiians today who practice *hula*, feel a Hawaiian spirituality with the *'āina* (land), and at the same time profess Christianity.

The Political-Economy of Hawai'i in the Twentieth Century

By the end of the 1800s, the interests informed by the missionary goals of civilizing and Christianizing the islands had combined with the interests of capitalists seeking to exploit the natural resources of the islands. With the overthrow of the monarchy in 1893 and the annexation of Hawai'i as a territory by the United

States five years later, American domination of the islands was virtually complete, although the shaping and institutionalization of a Western capitalist society continued into the twentieth century. The once-dominant hierarchical mode of production no longer existed; the older communal mode of production survived, as it does now, on the margins of the capitalist economy.

In twentieth-century Hawai'i, capitalism evolved from colonial capitalism into the now-dominant structures of corporate capitalism. The colonial mode, which lasted through the 1930s, was economically and politically dominated by sugar interests; the later corporate mode, by tourism. The major ideological distinction between the two is that corporate capitalism is hegemonic and colonial capitalism was not. Under the colonialism of the territorial government, an oligarchy of sugar interests exercised almost total political and economic control over the islands, but power was not based on popular consent; under corporate capitalism, even though economic and political power is more diffuse, the majority of the diverse ethnic groups and socioeconomic classes of Hawai'i accept the existing social structure as natural,[3] albeit not perfect.

Colonial Capitalism and the Politics of Race

The colonial structure depended on coercion, rather than consent, for social stability. The dominant material practices of the islands were not grounded in commonly shared systems of religion, culture, or language but were controlled by an ideology of plantation capitalism and racism ascribed to by a small but powerful minority. This ruling elite controlled the government and dominated the economic sphere. Subservient ethnic groups, for the most part plantation laborers, did not share, and in fact resented and resisted, the elite ideology. The basic underpinning of the dominating but not dominant ideology was a colonialist version of the Protestant ethic, a belief that hard work and competitive enterprise—by the right kind of people—was good not only for business but for the individual soul and the general welfare of the society. The success that came of such efforts was read as evidence of God's blessing and approval—a kind of Western version of the legitimization of *mana.*

There were fundamental contradictions in the colonial capitalist structure that the ideology of the dominant elite could not resolve for any but the elite themselves. The ideology of American capitalism and democracy and the rhetoric it inspired—that family line played no part in individual success, that anyone willing to work can succeed—was intolerably strained in the context of Hawai'i by the presence of dispossessed Hawaiians on the one hand and the discriminatory treatment of "Asiatics" on the other. No matter how hard Asian migrants were willing to work and save, they were blocked from achieving the rewards promised by the capitalist ethic by the same people who preached thrift and hard work to the Hawaiians.

The contradictions posed by the Hawaiians' presence were resolved by practices of paternalism and a justifying rhetoric inscribed by assumptions of the "white man's burden" and the benefits extended by Western civilization to "less fortunate" (read *inferior*) races. This was the local colonial variation of a rhetoric that had been used in every colonial context to justify and rationalize the dispossession of indigenous peoples. In Hawai'i, this racial and imperialist ideology blamed the Hawaiians for their fate; their poor condition, including even their demographic diminishment and infertility was due to their seemingly inherent inability to act responsibly, their lack of moral fiber, and "improper living."[4] In other words, the Hawaiians themselves made it "necessary" for the Americans to overthrow a "degenerating monarchy," an act that also happened to fulfill the God-given Manifest Destiny of the United States.

There is destiny in our final assumption of authority in the Pacific Ocean, in the recognition—forced from us by the natural sequence of our own acts—of the laws of commercial gravity, which we had ignored so stubbornly and for so long.

Americans brought commerce, civilization, education, prosperity to Hawaii. Was there not, indeed, warrant for giving this island colony the fuller benefits of annexation?

And what of the native? . . . There has been so much maudlin sentiment expended on him and such bias exhibited in discussion on this subject, it will be instructive, perhaps interesting, to have a glance at facts. Hysterical writers declare the native has lost all his belongings except his dark eyes and his passion for flowers: that his patrimony has been squandered, and finally his country taken from him. . . . There is nothing so obtrusive in the written history of Hawaiian life as the contrast between the harsh treatment of the natives by their own rulers and their kind treatment by the whites.[5]

If the course of history did not appear to have worked to the benefit of the Hawaiians, whose right was it to question the natural "gravity" of capitalism? The most that could be expected on the part of those in control was patient understanding and charitable actions to alleviate the "natives' plight."

The ideology of paternalism was practiced through patronage and a variety of charitable actions (foundations and trusts, as well as programs designed to assimilate and "rehabilitate" the Hawaiians). The low expectations and goals of educational programs, which stressed trade and vocational training, were shaped by American suppositions about the capabilities of Hawaiians and what they could be expected—or what was appropriate for them— to achieve. But, at the same time, the American territorial government was dependent on Hawaiians to staff various lower-level government jobs. For instance, in 1927 Hawaiians made up most of the fire department and all of the police department. As Davianna McGregor explains:

This led to a curious alliance between a large portion of the Hawaiian community, led by the native landed elite and the Big Five within the Republican Party. . . . the alliance was held together through government patronage, secure jobs on ranches and plantations, and anti-immigrant prejudices. . . . Through 1935, Hawaiians held almost a third of the public service jobs, although they comprised only 15 per cent of the population. Hawaiians who chose to accommodate American rule and collaborate with the Big Five enjoyed relatively privileged positions in the economy.[6]

While some urban Hawaiians were given a place in the dominant society through the 1930s, the other half of the Hawaiian population remained outside the dominant social structure, living in rural areas and surviving as marginal farmers within the traditional relationships of the old communal social structure.

In 1921, the U.S. Congress passed the Homestead Land Act, which set aside land for Hawaiians under long-term leases. But the intent of Congress was nullified by the sugar interests that protected productive lands for their own use. They allocated marginal lands ill suited for agriculture to the Hawaiians; later, some of these lands became prime sites used or leased by the state for airports and tourist development. The Homestead Act was of symbolic benefit to those in power who were able to point to constructive action on their part for the natives. Because of the way Home Lands were administered, Hawaiians were unable to use most of the land and could be blamed again by the paternalistic *haole*-controlled government for their inability to use land intelligently and industriously. In fact, more than half of the homestead land was either leased by the territorial government to non-Hawaiians or used for state purposes. Little of the remaining land was ever provided with the necessary infrastructure (electricity, sewage, roads, etc.) for home development. In seventy years, only three thousand families received homestead leases, accounting for only thirty thousand acres of the one hundred eighty-seven thousand put in the trust. In 1983, seven thousand families were on the waiting list; in 1990, almost twenty thousand families were waiting.[7] As a result, few Hawaiians have ever benefited from the

Homestead Land Act. Once a symbol of beneficence, the act, and the Department of Hawaiian Home Lands that administers it, is a continuing source of embarrassment for the state and federal governments.[8] In addition to homestead land, Hawaiians are supposed to benefit from two other land bases: ceded lands set aside under the Hawaii Admission Act and Bishop Estate lands whose sole purpose is to generate revenue to educate native Hawaiians. Like the Hawaiian Home Lands, the ceded lands and the Bishop Estate lands have primarily served the interests of politicians and developers—often one and the same in Hawai'i.[9]

The presence of Chinese, Japanese, Filipino, and other groups of Asian immigrant labor posed more difficult ideological contradictions than the Hawaiians. Because these Asians were brought to Hawai'i to work on sugar plantations, they were at the center of the islands' economy and therefore essential to the production of sugar and the reproduction of the social structure. Their dissatisfactions were impossible to ignore; many left the confines of the plantations for other jobs or to set up small businesses in Honolulu and smaller towns in the islands as soon as their contracts were up. But most stayed and demanded better pay and living conditions on the plantations.

Throughout the period of colonial capitalism, the ruling *haole* elite defined their practices as synonymous with the social good and natural order. Acting within their understanding of government and still-prevailing nineteenth-century notions about progress and race, the elite fashioned a government apparatus that functioned as an arm of the sugar industry. The territorial government reacted immediately and consistently to meet the needs of sugar production, passing and enforcing laws that regulated the resources and relations of production as the industry dictated. For instance, when it became apparent that too many workers were leaving the plantations at the expiration of their contracts, the legislature passed a law that excluded Asians from various nonagricultural occupations; later, a law was passed that prohibited "Asiatic" labor from employment on public works.[10]

Plantation control was reinforced by practices that structured occupations by race. In 1904, the Hawaii Sugar Planters Association (HSPA) adopted a resolution stating that all skilled positions should be filled by Americans or those eligible for American citizenship. Because of existing immigration laws, this meant Asians could not hold skilled jobs on the plantations. In 1911, another resolution was passed by the HSPA that reserved skilled and semiskilled positions for Hawaiians and whites.[11] A self-serving and racist rhetoric held that whites were "constitutionally and temperamentally unfitted for labor in a tropical climate," while Asians and "brown" men were "peculiarly adapted to the exactions of tropical labor" and could serve as satisfactory and "permanent" field workers.[12] Within the workforce, plantation owners made other racial and ethnic distinctions: Portuguese and other immigrant whites, such as Germans, were almost always hired as overseers, but if a Japanese became an overseer, he was paid one-third the wage. Japanese cane cutters were paid more than Filipino cane cutters (99 cents a day and 69 cents a day respectively), and white carpenters earned more than Japanese carpenters ($4.36 a day versus $1.28 a day). These and other distinctions by race reinforced racial divisions and constructed a social hierarchy within the plantation system,[13] producing ethnic and class divisions that were maintained by the racial ideology of colonialism.

The territorial government's blatantly racist policies were sometimes blocked by the federal government, but increasingly these coercive practices were challenged by the growing "intransigence" of labor itself. The disenfranchisement of Japanese aliens, the largest ethnic group in the 1920s, negated any political threat that they might muster at the ballot boxes—at least until the second generation (who were American citizens by birth) reached voting age.[14] But as the size of the labor force increased, the power of labor grew, winning increased wages and better working conditions from the sugar planters. There were major, prolonged, and relatively well-organized strikes in 1909 (all Japanese) and 1920 (Japanese and Filipino) that attempted to alter the relations of production, with the workers forcing recognition of themselves as human actors, rather than as commodities in the production of sugar. While the planters' association was able to break both strikes, the demanded benefits were conceded in practice shortly after the strikes ended.

By the 1920s, class consciousness and a working-class ethic were clearly emerging with demands for better wages replacing earlier complaints about mistreatment by plantation managers and foremen. As the strength of labor grew, the efforts of planters to secure compliance by physical or economic coercion were replaced by a paternalism that sought to develop a sense of loyalty and "family" community within the plantation structure. Gradually, the plantation economy was transformed by organized labor into a form of welfare capitalism at the plantation level.[15] Even now, Hawai'i is unique in the wages and benefits earned by agricultural workers. Although most of the descendants of plantation workers work in nonagricultural jobs, Hawai'i has remained a strong prolabor state with union jobs now primarily in hotels, construction industries, and state and local government entities.

Corporate Capitalism and the Politics of Paradise

The entrance into the islands of mainland labor unions in the 1930s, the outbreak of war in 1941, the demands of second-generation Japanese-Americans (working through the Democratic party) for a piece of the political action after 1945, the development of large-scale tourism with the initiation of jet service to and from the islands, intense land speculation and hotel development after statehood—all were forces that led to the demise of colonial capitalism in Hawai'i. In particular, the emergence of tourism as the dominant industry integrated Hawai'i into the global structures of corporate capitalism.[16] The rise of these new economic and political forces was matched by a parallel demise in the political and economic status of Hawaiians. The *haole*-dominated Republican party that had given patronage jobs to Hawaiians was replaced by the Japanese-American-dominated

Democratic party. Increasing job competition from Asian laborers leaving the plantations and a new wave of immigrants from the U.S. mainland led to decreases in the numbers of Hawaiians holding permanent wage-earning jobs, particularly in such white-collar occupations as government service and teaching. But it was primarily the rapid and intense development of land for tourism and the subsequent displacement of Hawaiians from urban enclaves and rural communities that had supported a still somewhat traditional lifestyle that undercut the social well-being of Hawaiians, marginalized them politically and socially, and alienated them psychologically.

The colonial capitalism of the prewar years was crucially different from today's corporate capitalism. The existing social structure is now reproduced by the day-to-day practices of the people who live in the islands. Although the politics and ideology of race that dominated the era of colonial capitalism are suppressed by the politics and rhetoric of development, progress, and statehood, ethnicity continues to play a significant role in Hawai'i's electoral politics and social relations. But ethnicity, while important in political elections, is contained within the hegemonic structures of power and the ideology of Hawai'i as a multicultural paradise. With the exception of Hawaiian political activism, ethnic differences are no longer a threat to the reproduction of the social structure. Nevertheless, contradictions in the social structure are becoming increasingly evident in unequal allocations of resources and the growing disparity between low-income tourist jobs and the high cost of living in Hawai'i. Recent astronomical increases in land and housing costs (a doubling between 1980 and 1990), caused primarily by a spurt of outside investment, mainly from Japan, have created economic problems not only for low-income workers but for the middle class as well. A headline in the *Honolulu Advertiser* of October 26, 1991, read: *Price of Paradise: 34% Higher Than Mainland.*

Ownership and control of land remain the ultimate measure of political power in the islands. Hotel development, agriculture, housing, recreational development, and environmentalists' demands for open space and the preservation of natural resources are contending claims on land. As the twentieth century comes to a close, new forces have become part of the continuing politics of land, including outside investors (now primarily from Asia), geothermal developers, and high-tech entrepreneurs. These new players are joining environmentalists, Hawaiians, the homeless and near-homeless, and the "visitor" industry (a euphemism for tourism) in intense debates over how Hawai'i's land should be used.

Hawaiian Music and the Industries of Culture

At the same time the political economy of the islands was undergoing capitalist reformation, Hawaiian music was being transformed by the technologies and business practices of the early entertainment industries. We have already seen how chant and *hula* were transformed by Western influences during the 1800s; in the twentieth century, Hawaiian music was further changed by the recording industry and tourism.

In the first half of the present century, technological developments in record making and later radio broadcasting changed the ways in which music was produced, distributed, and enjoyed throughout the world. Wherever these new technologies were privately owned, music became a commodity and a new set of values and motivations were brought to its creation and performance. Within this new context of cultural production, Hawaiian music was reconstituted as something that could be marketed, sold to, and consumed by mass audiences—not only in Hawai'i but all over the world.

The other major industry of culture that changed the nature of Hawaiian music was tourism. Even in the late 1800s, Hawaiian culture was recognized as a resource for a potential visitor industry and Hawaiians as entertainers and an exotic presence that added to the lure of the islands. By the 1920s and 1930s, tourism had constructed enduring images of Hawaiians as happy-go-lucky beach boys, friendly bus drivers, smiling *lei* sellers, funny entertainers, or beautiful women performing an exotic and somewhat erotic form of dance—all were part of the heavily marketed image of Hawai'i.[17] Within these trivialized versions of Hawaiian culture, limited and defined roles existed for Hawaiians as service providers and entertainers. The racial ideology that still excluded Hawaiians from middle- and upper-echelon occupations carved a niche for them in tourism that made profitable use of their culture as well as their labor.

The Recording Industry

After the U.S. annexation of the islands and throughout the first few decades of the twentieth century, Americans were intensely interested in Hawai'i. A Hawaiian music craze swept the mainland as a result of the appearance of Hawaiian musicians at the Panama-Pacific International Exhibition in 1925 in San Francisco and a great Broadway hit of the 1920s, *Bird of Paradise*. At the same time, more and more mainlanders were visiting or moving to the islands. The recording and tourist industries worked to mutual benefit, each publicizing the other, both having a tremendous impact on the development and shape of Hawaiian music.

New forms of Hawaiian music were created that incorporated the stereotypes of Hawai'i into popular mainland music styles.[18] Hawaiian musicians such as Alfred Apaka and Sol Bright, and American Tin Pan Alley songwriters and performers, many of whom had never been to the islands, wrote and performed *hapa haole* music (popular music that combines Hawaiian words or themes with mainland music styles). Hawaiian (and self-styled Hawaiian) performers entertained in hotel ballrooms across the mainland and recorded "Hawaiian music" for large mainland recording companies: Victor, Columbia, and Decca. In the United States, *hapa haole* records outsold any other form of popular music. The major companies capitalized on the fad for Hawaiian music that peaked just before the Great Depression and then picked up again in the late 1930s. Sales were spurred by films such as Bing Crosby's *Waikiki Wedding* and the popular national radio program "Hawaii Calls." Hundreds of "Hawaiian" records were released: the 1939 Decca catalog showed 391 Hawaiian records; Victor had 189. Hawaiian music production by mainland companies (later joined by small local companies) continued through the 1950s, although production was disrupted during World War II. With the arrival of rock 'n' roll in the late 1950s and 1960s, interest in Hawaiian music faded, and the mainland recording industry finally dropped the category from their catalogs. The small local industry continued to produce records primarily for the tourist market and a limited local market—static markets until the Hawaiian Renaissance began in the mid-1970s.

Although the local recording industry operates within the legal, commercial, and professional codes of the national music industry (e.g., copyright laws, royalties, and performing rights), it is relatively independent of the mainland industry in terms of ownership and distribution—a situation that has advantages and disadvantages for local musicians, particularly those seeking to enter the mainland market. Still, the styles and technologies of music production developed by the global music industry strongly influence the sounds and forms of local music production. The ultimate measure of musical success for many local musicians is to break into the mainland, the Japanese, or other large external markets. That desire shapes local music in subtle and sometimes not-so-subtle ways. Even musicians who want to stay in Hawai'i and perform for small but appreciative local audiences are affected by market forces.

The development of the music industry in Hawai'i illustrates how the production of music or art of any kind is affected by market conditions. In Hawai'i, as elsewhere, commercial codes of production have become generalized and internalized. Musicians competing for capital, sales, and audiences in a market where outside tastes must be taken into consideration make complex compromises (often not consciously) between market demands and their creative desires.[19] For instance, Peter Moon, a major figure in contemporary Hawaiian music, is fully aware of the need to satisfy a diverse market; he produces records that have a mix of local and mainland music styles, saying that this is necessary to ensure enough sales to make recording music in Hawai'i profitable.[20]

In the 1970s, the pull of the mainland music industry was countered by the availability of technologies of production and dissemination (notably audio cassettes) that made relatively low-cost recordings possible. A number of small local recording companies entered the market during this period, and many musicians started their own labels, producing contemporary and traditional Hawaiian music for enthusiastic local audiences with capital raised from their own funds or from friends and family. During the mid-1970s, the production and sale of local recordings was very strong. Some albums sold close to one hundred thousand units; previously, five thousand was considered a successful sale. Contemporary musicians such as Peter Moon, the Cazimero Brothers, Gabby Pahinui, and the Sons of Hawaii created a new sound that combined folk, rock, country, and Hawaiian music with added amplification and more instruments. In 1975, only five Hawaiian albums were released; in 1977, fifty-three were released.[21] The peak year for record production was 1978; 110 albums were released and approximately a quarter of a million units were sold, generating from $1 million to $6 million for the local industry. Although record production slowed in the 1980s, it remained fairly steady with from thirty-five to fifty albums produced each year. The 1990s may be a period of renewed recording activity. On the 1992 preliminary ballot for the Nā Hōkū Hanohano awards, 90 LPs, cassettes or compact discs were listed under "album of the year." They ran the gamut from jazz, pop, comedy and religious music to contemporary and traditional Hawaiian. As is true anywhere, when it comes to keeping track of popular music production, it is almost impossible to maintain a complete census of musicians and their musical creations. It is not clear whether the 1992 output reflects a real increase, or better ways of identifying local output, or some of both.[22] In spite of problems, Hawai'i's local recording industry remains an example of what many countries would like to achieve—a locally owned industry that serves as an outlet for traditional styles of music (broadly defined) and that offers contemporary musicians of all styles of music a system within which they can produce their own music relatively free of the economic and creative controls of the mainstream music industry.

Tourism and Hawaiian Music

Tourism has played a major role in determining musical practices in Hawai'i. In the specific arenas where Hawaiian music is performed primarily for tourists, conventions of form constrain, shape, and determine the content of performance and exclude anything but the most commercially "packaged" acts. These conventions and codes, determined by the political economies of tourism and advertising, say that only the most easily consumable kinds of Hawaiian music can find a place in Waikīkī.

The perceptions that outsiders have of Hawaiians, and even to some extent the perceptions that Hawaiians have of themselves, have largely been constructed by the tourist industry. These images have been further disseminated by advertising and broadcast and film media throughout the world. Much of popular Hawaiian music has reinforced these stereotypes. The following song by part-Hawaiian composer Eaton Magoon, Jr., was number one on the local hit parade in 1946. It was a time when American servicemen and -women were returning from the war, and the song became a favorite jukebox selection in Honolulu. The lyrics express the theme of statehood and the stereotype of Hawaiians as lazy but happy people:

Mama don't scold me, I no go work today
Down there in Iwilei in the pineapple cannery.
Mama don't scold me, I bring a *lei* for you,
I sing all day for you, the songs of Hawai'i.

Fish and *poi*, fish and *poi*, all I need is fish and *poi*.
Sunshine free, Waikīkī, no care tomorrow.

Sister Bell, dress up swell, dance the *hula* in the big hotel.
Shake this way, shake that way, no care tomorrow.
Mama don't scold her, someday she catch a boy
She bring him fish and *poi* at the pineapple cannery.

Mama no feel bad, someday I sure make good.
Hawai'i get Statehood, make President maybe.

Fish and *poi*, fish and *poi*, all I need is fish and *poi*.
Need no more from the store, no care tomorrow.
Fish and *poi*, fish and *poi*, all day long eat fish and *poi*.
Big *'opu* [stomach], no *huhu* [worry], no care tomorrow.

A kind of symbiotic relationship exists between tourism and local music, with tourism providing jobs for musicians and a market for records, while Hawaiian music is a resource that enhances the attraction of Hawai'i as a tourist destination and entertains tourists once they are here. Although the relationship is symbiotic, power resides with the hotels and other businesses that hire performers; this inequality is an effect of the structure of the tourist and music industries and of the nature of music production and performance within that context. With the exception of a few big-name entertainers who work under long-term contracts with major hotels, for example, Don Ho at the Hilton Hawaiian Village, Danny Kaleikini at the Kahala Hilton, and the Brothers Cazimero at the Royal Hawaiian, local musicians are poorly paid and intermittently employed, unable as performers to make enough money to support themselves and their families. Although there is an active local of the national musicians union in Hawai'i, union membership is perceived as a mixed blessing. If the union pushes pay scales higher than hotels are willing to pay, nonunion players are hired instead, jobs are eliminated, or the number of performances are cut back. In other words, the union as well as individual musicians have little bargaining leverage because the demands of the tourist industry for entertainment are elastic, while the supply of musicians is not.[23]

Tourism and Paradise: Appropriating Hawaiian Culture

Tourism is pervasive in the islands. Little about island life is not in some way affected by tourism—certainly Hawaiian music is. Tourism is more than the large percentage of jobs and businesses that depend on it; more than the political clout of an industry that generates close to 40 percent of the state's gross product;[24] more than the physical presence of tourists on crowded streets, highways, beaches, and parks; more than the allocation of limited land and water resources for hotel and golf-course development. It is all these realities plus a more subtle presence that operates at the level of sign, symbol, and social consciousness.

Tourism is an industry based on image; its overriding concern is to construct, through multiple representations of paradise, an imaginary Hawai'i that entices the outsider to place himself or herself into this symbol-defined space. In the process of image and sign construction, Hawaiian culture and particularly Hawaiian music are used and positioned in ways that give new meanings to their presentation and performance. For instance, Hawaiian Airlines had an advertising campaign that used the slogan "We are Hawaiian." In the print media and on television, ads presented an exotic, primitive and romantic version of Hawai'i, in one showing *malo*-clad men dancing before a flickering fire in a cavelike setting and in another, a beautiful woman on a deserted beach.

In the setting of a hotel *lū'au*, more important than the food or seeing a performance of Hawaiian *hula* is the image constructed for the tourist of participating in an exotic experience. This is what Baudrillard sees in postcapitalism as the "political economy of the sign," the complex relationships that reverse all values so that ultimately we are really consuming signs that become definitions of ourselves. For instance, in the act of cultural consumption (attending a Hawaiian show), the exchange value of money (what it cost to be there) and the symbolic value of *hula* (the performance itself) are transmuted into sign value (the image of one's self that comes from being entertained by Hawaiians in Hawai'i— "enjoying the vacation of a lifetime in beautiful Waikīkī").[25]

But Baudrillard's concept of the political economy of the sign extends beyond the products and experiences sold to tourists; it is the total environment of the islands that is ultimately marketed as the tourist experience. Almost everything in Hawai'i communicates through a system of codes that tourism, and the public and private institutions that support tourism, have constructed over years of selling Hawai'i as paradise. Within the semiotic logic of Hawai'i as the ultimate tourist destination, the totality of the islands (the sun and the ocean, the green of the sugarcane, the multiracial society going about its daily activities) is offered to the consuming gaze of tourists. The production of paradise is an all-encompassing code that revalues everything in the islands, imposing social relations and codes of behavior on the total structure of the islands. It is the logic that says locals cannot surf where tour boats want to go, that local residents must suffer the noise of sightseeing helicopters or the fumes of tour buses, that golf courses are more productive than agriculture.

Tourism supports most of the island population in one way or another, although not grandly for most; approximately one-third of jobs statewide are directly or indirectly generated by tourism.[26] The vital signs of the industry are continuously and anxiously monitored and reported in local papers: the rise and fall in the numbers of tourists, hotel occupancy rates, daily spending averages of mainland and Japanese tourists—all are indices of the total well-being of the islands. Protecting the fragile resource of the "*aloha* spirit" is a concern of the industry and hence the state.[27] Since tourism is dependent on image, tourists are as easily dissuaded from a destination by reports of crime and social conflict as they are lured to it by images of fun and romance. For that reason, crimes against tourists are often taken more seriously than similar crimes against local residents. For the same reason, the tourist industry mounts public relations campaigns directed at local residents, the message being that tourism supports us all and therefore we should be hospitable to our "visitors."

A recent campaign by the state-funded Hawaii Visitors Bureau is an example of how the tourist industry seeks to preserve Hawaiian culture because it is a marketable resource. Big ads addressed to local businesses were placed in newspapers. Under a picture of a *hula* dancer in a grass skirt, one ad read:

> Keep it Hawai'i. Hula is good for business. Sometimes we forget, but visitors to our islands have invested a lot of time— and money—to get here. For them, it's a dream that's finally come true. So let's show them a thing or two. Your business can add to the magic of Hawai'i by sharing examples of our heritage and traditions. Hawaiian music, a hula demonstration, or the simple gift of a flower can create lasting memories for visitors. Better still, your efforts give back to the community by helping preserve the true essence of Hawai'i.

Today, a number of powerful interests dominate the social structure of the islands, but it is a different set of actors from the ones that dominated Hawai'i from the early 1900s through the 1960s. The most notable change has to do with the virtual disappearance of the Big Five, the major companies that controlled the islands' plantation system. All but one, Alexander and Baldwin, moved to the mainland or were sold off in whole or in part in the 1980s. Some of the current economic and political leaders have their base in the remnants of the old colonial social order; others emerged as part of the postwar power structure (an alliance of the Democratic party, labor unions, land developers, and tourism). At the beginning of the 1990s, new players are entering the field, the most obvious being foreign—mostly Japanese— developers and investors. Tourism remains the engine of the economy, accounting for some 40 percent of the gross state product. This excessive dependency on a fragile and volatile industry is worrisome to many, and the government has tried to diversify the economy by taking advantage of Hawai'i's proximity to expanding financial and trading centers in Asia. On the one hand, the state is trying to construct a new image for Hawai'i as the financial, commercial, and technological center of the Pacific; on the other, it still puts millions of dollars into advertising Hawai'i as a paradise of pleasure.[28]

The Politics of Culture—Hawai'i Style

The notion of pluralism has been an ideologically useful concept in American politics, and probably nowhere more so than in Hawai'i. Balancing ethnicity and cultural diversity is an art in Hawai'i. Each of the many cultures of the islands—Japanese, Chinese, Filipino, Hawaiian, Korean, Samoan, Portuguese, and so on—is allocated a proper place in the discourse and displays of culture. In state-run festivals, in state and local arts agencies, in museums, and in parades, each ethnic group is given time and space to represent itself in predefined ways—with dance, art, crafts, literature, films, and so forth. State grants to artists and the various ethnic cultural organizations are carefully balanced along with educational programs and cultural studies at all levels of education. The Year of the Japanese, the Year of the Chinese, and the Year of the Hawaiian have been celebrated; during each of these years, histories of hardship and struggle have been uncovered and then brought within the enveloping, hegemonic discourse of Hawai'i as a multiethnic plurality, a "rainbow" of people coexisting in social harmony. History and continuing social inequities are rendered harmless, transformed into exhibits, entertainment, and spectacles of ethnic food and customs.

This whole discourse of culture is defined along Western notions of ethnicity. The only culture in the islands that does not have an ethnic studies program, that does not have a year celebrating its arrival, that is not featured in special museum celebrations is Western culture. Even though the *haole* population does not constitute a majority of the islands' people and its people are as foreign as any of the Asian cultures that now reside here, Western culture—specifically American culture—is so dominant it has no need to call attention to itself or construct itself as different; it is simply the taken-for-granted touchstone against which all other cultures construct their unique ethnic identities.

Hawaiians and the Politics of Culture

A hegemonic Western culture dominates the islands, but it does not totally control the discourse of culture. Although Hawaiian culture is now, in effect, a subculture of the hegemonic culture, it refuses to be satisfied with the allocations of space, time, and roles the dominant culture would give it. Hawaiian culture is both residual in its ties to the past and oppositional in its critique of the existing social structure of the islands and its projections of the future.[29]

Hawaiians are the only major ethnic group still significantly outside of, and at odds with, the hegemonic structure. Excluded from the main economic and political arenas before World War II, Hawaiians had little involvement in shaping the social structure of the islands after the war. In the 1970s, the discontent of Hawaiians surfaced at the same time minorities and women throughout the United States were protesting social inequalities. Since then, Hawaiians have mounted a sustained opposition within a number of political arenas—the courts, the university, and the legislative and administrative bodies of the state and counties—on a range of issues affecting Hawaiians as a cultural group and their environment and lifestyle. The Hawaiian Renaissance was a period of political protest and action and increasing ethnic awareness. At one level, this was manifested in a resurgence of interest in Hawaiian culture: chant and *hula*, contemporary Hawaiian music, outrigger canoeing, the Pacific voyaging expeditions of the Hōkūle'a, and so on. Hawaiians demanded Hawaiian-language programs from preschool to university level and succeeded in establishing the Hawaiian Studies Program at the University of Hawaii. Through the 1970s and into the 1980s, many demonstrations took place over land development and forced evictions of Hawaiians from private, county, and state-owned lands. At the Constitutional Convention in 1978, radical young Hawaiians and their political allies succeeded in establishing the Office of Hawaiian Affairs (OHA) as a semiautonomous government office.[30]

It is always difficult to talk about another culture's beliefs and political goals without essentializing. Describing "the Hawaiians" in the past, before Western contact, when Hawaiian culture constituted the totality of island culture, is problematic enough for twentieth-century historians; it is much more so now when "the Hawaiians" are one of several cultures in Hawai'i, and most are affiliated by circumstance and blood with other social and ethnic groups.[31] Their Hawaiianess is only part of their cultural and political identities, and like all of us who live in postmodern Hawai'i, their constructs of self are multiple and shifting, encompassing various public and domestic roles and gender and class affiliations. It is clear from reading the local newspapers that contemporary Hawaiians ascribe to a range of cultural beliefs and practices and hold various positions on social issues, including sovereignty and other matters directly affecting their environmental, social, and cultural resources.

Most of the people who select their Hawaiian identity as their primary one for census takers have been politically mobilized since the early 1970s. They have protested the continuous encroachment of development throughout the islands and the obvious social and economic disparities that exist between the majority of Hawaiians and groups that have prospered from the appropriation of Hawaiian resources. Although there are many important business, cultural, and economic leaders from the Hawaiian community (including the current governor), virtually every social indicator (e.g., income, health and mortality, education, employment patterns, crime and incarceration rates) makes it clear that Hawaiians as an ethnic group are still excluded from the benefits of, and alienated by the effects of, development in Hawai'i. This was clearly documented in the 1983 studies commissioned by the federal government to examine Hawaiian claims for reparations to compensate for the illegal overthrow of the Hawaiian monarchy in 1893.[32]

Hawaiian demands are multiple, but most of them relate in one way or another to preservation of lifestyle and culture and control of land—the perennial political issue of the islands and one that has profound cultural and emotional significance for most Hawaiians. Out of a deep concern for maintaining their culture and identity, Hawaiians argue for use of ceded lands, for housing and infrastructure on Hawaiian Home Lands, for securing legal standing vis-à-vis the State of Hawai'i, for legislation concerning blood quantum and access to social services, for protection of traditional fishing and gathering rights, and for maintaining a significant Hawaiian presence in the few remaining areas where Hawaiian culture is still closely linked to a sense of place and community.

Hawaiian sovereignty and geothermal development on the Big Island are two issues over which Hawaiian groups have used a discourse of culture in political struggles. The notion of sovereignty challenges the taken-for-granted acceptance of Hawai'i as a state within the United States. Mainstream histories of Hawai'i frame statehood as a ballot-box issue that was overwhelmingly approved and greeted by island residents. This hegemonic discourse of democracy obscures the history of Hawaiian alienation and statehood as the outcome of a long process of domination.

Hawaiian sovereignty is a goal of several Hawaiian groups, but what degree of sovereignty and under what governance is open to debate. The common goal that unites many of these groups is land rights. While only a few groups believe that Hawai'i will ever become a totally sovereign nation again, there is the possibility of Hawaiian control over a portion of island lands including ceded lands and Hawaiian Home Lands. For instance, Ka Lāhui (the Nation of Hawai'i), organized by a group of prominent Hawaiian activists in 1987 and with an enrollment of about 12,000 in 1992, advocates direct negotiation with the federal government for settlement of outstanding grievances and for recognition of Hawaiians as a "nation within a nation" with voting and citizenship open only to Hawaiians.[33] The most readily apparent models for Hawaiian sovereignty are those created for American Indians. But when American Indians are evoked, either to secure benefits for Hawaiians under federal Native American programs or as governmental models of limited sovereignty, Hawaiians are discursively positioned as "Native Americans." It may be that sovereignty under such models is better than nothing, and the intended economic and social benefits are certainly important to disadvantaged Hawaiians, but the symbolic tradeoff of being labeled "Native Americans," rather than Hawaiians, is a significant concession of identity. Also, to talk about sovereignty within American legal definitions of government and relations between governmental entities reproduces dominant ideological frameworks and classifying schemes. As a result, even what first seem radical challenges to established structures of power are drawn into the practices and constraints of legal and legislative discourses and thereby normalized and made ideologically "grammatical."[34]

The fight over geothermal development on the Big Island also shows how complex issues are inscribed by mechanisms of political, economic, and intellectual power. The geothermal development plan calls for several wells to be drilled on the slopes of Kīlauea volcano. These wells are to produce up to 500 megawatts of geothermal-generated electric power that could be transported through overland and underwater cable to the islands of Maui and Oʻahu. The geothermal debates have generated an alliance of economic and political interests in favor of the development that include labor and big business, most of the state legislators, and the governor, while dividing groups that usually are together on cultural and environmental issues.[35] Various groups have sent forth their experts to do battle with other experts—economists and financial experts, geologists, botanists, public health doctors, air-quality experts, volcanologists, energy engineers, meterologists, and so on. Natural scientists from the same disciplines have been enlisted by opposing sides to talk about native and alien species of birds and plants, biodiversity, the protection of rain forests, alternative energy, and global warming.

Many Hawaiians have been in the front ranks of the opposition to geothermal development. The Pele Defense Fund, the Big Island Rainforest Action Group, various Puna district community groups and the Office of Hawaiian Affairs have been fighting geothermal development in the courts, the legislature, and in front of bulldozers. Their opposition tactics have included informational meetings throughout the islands, demonstrations at the area of proposed development, and large ads in mainland newspapers including the *New York Times* and the *Wall Street Journal*.

Hawaiians have argued against the geothermal project on all dimensions—health, land values, costs to consumers, rain-forest protection, and endangered species. They have, however, focused their appeal on Hawaiian culture: respect for Hawaiian religion and the area as the home of the Goddess Pele, traditional rights of access to the Wao Kele O Puna rain forest, and the area as a place of Hawaiian spiritual renewal. In this discourse of culture and spirituality, Hawaiians are on their strongest yet weakest ground. In the areas of science, ecology, finance, and health, anti-geothermal arguments are accepted as rational and legitimate, and state legislators are accustomed to deciding issues based on appeals to social costs and benefits for "the common good." Even on the abstract terrain of "tradition and lifestyle," Hawaiian concerns have generally been conceded legitimacy; protecting Hawaiian culture is seen as worthwhile, both to compensate Hawaiians for what they have lost and to "preserve the *aloha* spirit" as a resource for tourism. The discourse of Hawaiian culture also has its recognized specialists—anthropologists, archaeologists, museum experts, Hawaiian Studies faculty—who are called as expert witnesses in court hearings and public debates, interviewed by the press, and sometimes contracted to carry out social-impact studies before development plans are approved. For instance, based on archaeological studies, a major highway was redesigned to avoid ancient *heiau* remains, and hotel developers no longer can expect to build over major Hawaiian burial sites.

But when Hawaiians contest geothermal development on the basis of religion—when they take Pele from the realm of Hawaiian folklore and talk of her as a goddess that Hawaiians worship, and when they talk about chant and *hula* as religious rites—Hawaiians move outside the boundaries of Western rational discourse, and this discourse of religion makes the majority of listeners uncomfortable. Such social institutions as the legislature, government agencies, and the courts are willing to make some concessions on the basis of Hawaiian culture—its protection and maintenance—but not on the basis of Hawaiian religion. Pele is accepted within the context of tourism entertainment or anthropology or folklore because those are discursive fields where the exotic has been normalized by Western discourses of the Other.

A truly hegemonic society is always adjusting to and accommodating alternative and even oppositional meanings, values, and practices. The very fact that Hawaiian sovereignty is argued within the rules, codes, and assumptions of U.S. legislative and legal systems and that declarations of Hawaiian sovereignty are presented within documents that are models of Western constitutions makes conceptualizations of Hawaiian independence problematic. It is too early to say whether the political struggles of pro-sovereignty Hawaiians will force significant structural change, or whether their demands will be ideologically accommodated by the dominant hegemony "reforming" itself in response to social demands and giving the semblance of responsiveness without actually affecting the distribution of power.

Chant and *hula* have been employed by competing myths of Hawai'i. Myths shift and change as their symbols and signs are enlisted by competing representations of realities. For Hawaiians prior to the intrusion of the West, *hula* and chant were the center of ideological practice and representation. They represented and legitimated the religious and political totality of Hawai'i. They were performative commentaries and declarations that constituted a total system of meaning.

With Western contact and the colonization of the islands, chant and *hula* were redefined as each new contingent of outsiders encountered Hawaiians and their culture. For early voyagers such as Captains Cook and Vancouver and the natural scientists and artists who sailed with them, chant and *hula* were seen as signifiers of an exotic people. For the missionaries, the performance of chant and particularly *hula* were signs of people living in darkness. For Kalākaua and the Hawaiians seeking to protect their sovereignty from Western encroachment and domination, chant and *hula* were symbols of Hawaiian pride and sovereignty. For the tourist industry, chant and *hula* and the new forms of Hawaiian music are commodities that can be sold and used to market the islands. For the tourists that come to Hawai'i, Hawaiian music is entertainment and evidence of an experience in paradise that can be captured on film.

In the 1970s and 1980s, Hawaiian music became something else again: an important symbol for a new Hawaiian political movement. The resurgence of political awareness and ethnic pride among Hawaiians was expressed by an intense interest in and practice of Hawaiian music. In the 1970s, local musicians such as Gabby Pahinui and the Sunday Manoa began performing outside Waikīkī in small clubs and restaurants, in open-air concerts, and at protest rallies. Hawaiian music also served as a symbol of opposition for other groups disenchanted with the rapid development of the islands. In the late 1980s and into the 1990s, the explicit political content of contemporary Hawaiian music is again becoming more evident. As Hawaiians anticipate 1993, one hundred years after the overthrow of the Hawaiian monarchy, music is being written and composed that expresses the frustrations of many Hawaiians and the political aspirations for greater, if not total control over the Hawaiian islands. For instance, at a pro-sovereignty rally held in 1988, Hawaiian activists sang Kaulana Nā Pua (Famous Are the Children), the protest song written in 1893 after Queen Lili'uokalani was removed from her throne (see the lyrics in Chapter Five).[36] The 1992 Nā Hōkū Hanohano award for Song of the Year went to Henry Kapono, Israel Kamakawiwo'ole, Cyril Pahinui and Roland Cazimero for "Broken Promise," an anthem to Hawaiian pride and sovereignty. At the ceremony, Henry Kapono said, "It's directed a lot to the government; it's hiding things from us. . . . I've won more than a dozen Hokus but this one means the most to me, because I'm a Hawaiian and I'm proud and I finally made a full circle to realize it."[37] At the same ceremony, the group Olomana received the award for the best contemporary Hawaiian album for its *E Mau Ana Ka Ha'aheo* (Enduring Pride). One of the songs on the album, written by Jerry Santos, speaks of Queen Lili'uokalani walking in her garden and of the "sovereignty our people call today." In effect, the Hawaiian political movement has again reconstituted and reappropriated Hawaiian music as a symbol of a recovered history, a representation of contemporary Hawaiian identity, a vehicle of public protest, and as a voice for Hawaiian sovereignty. The performance of Hawaiian music has taken on an explicit political message by practice, if not always by content, becoming part of a politicized discourse about Hawai'i that challenges the dominant myth of paradise.

The music of Hawai'i can be read as an intertext.[38] As the ideological, economic, and political structure of the islands have changed and continue to change, so have the forms of Hawaiian music. Chant, *hula,* and the hybrid forms that developed after contact with the West will continue to change in instrumentation, style, and content; in the definition of what constitutes Hawaiian music; and in the motivations for music creation and performance. Today, in its totality, Hawaiian music is a mixture of traditional and modern music (*hula* and chant, hymns, *hapa haole* music, jazz, rock 'n' roll); religious beliefs (Hawaiian and Christian); different cultural experiences (Hawaiian, Western, Asian); myths (precontact and ad agency created); economic constraints and incentives; and political ideologies. Hawaiian music continues to evolve as each new wave of outside cultural and social influence sweeps the islands. It is an intertext where Hawai'i, the West, and the social context of the present continuously interact to construct, deconstruct, and reconstruct the myths of Hawai'i.

Notes

Chapter One

1. The description of the Kodak Hula Show is based on my observations in the spring of 1986.

2. The term *haole* originally meant any foreigner; it is now used to designate a Caucasian.

3. Not all the dancers in the Kodak Hula Show, or any other tourist show, are Hawaiian. Some are "locals," which usually refers to residents of the state, who may be any combination of Japanese, Chinese, Hawaiian, Samoan, Filipino, *haole*, and other racial and ethnic backgrounds. The performers need only be skilled dancers and fit the show's semblance of Polynesia.

4. The stands of the Kodak Hula Show seat 3,000 people, roughly one-third of whom have cameras. It has been estimated that 12,000 photos are taken at each show. Only Disney World and Disneyland sell more film than the Kodak Hula Show. "After Fifty Years, Hula Show Still Clicks," *Honolulu Advertiser*, March 7, 1987, A3.

5. This discussion of myth draws on Roland Barthes, *Mythologies*, trans. Annette Lavers (New York: Hill and Wang, 1972), 109–159.

6. Ibid., 151.

7. Ibid., 142–143.

8. Janice Otaguro, "The Rebels of Hula," *Honolulu* 26, no. 5 (November 1991): 100.

9. Wendell P. K. Silva, "Introduction," in *Nana I Na Loea* (Look to the Hula resources) (Honolulu: Kalihi-Palama Culture & Arts Society, 1984), vi.

10. Otaguro, "Rebels of Hula," 102.

11. Silva, *Nana I Na Loea*, 30.

12. Ibid., 45.

13. Ibid., 8.

14. Ibid., 66.

15. The field of anthropology has been politicized in debates over relationships of power inherent in practices of fieldwork and ethnographic writing and the historical and contemporary links between

Western domination of the Third World and anthropology. Key texts in this debate include Edward Said, *Orientalism* (New York: Random House, 1978); James Clifford and George E. Marcus, *Writing Culture: The Poetics and Politics of Ethnography* (Berkeley: University of California Press, 1986); James Clifford, *The Predicament of Culture: Twentieth Century Ethnography, Literature, and Art* (Cambridge, Mass.: Harvard University Press, 1988). For an example of this debate in the Pacific, particularly in Hawai'i, see Roger M. Keesing, "Creating the Past: Custom and Identity in the Contemporary Pacific," *Contemporary Pacific: A Journal of Island Affairs* 1, nos. 1 and 2 (Spring and Fall 1989): 19–39; Haunani-Kay Trask, "Natives and Anthropologists: The Colonial Struggle," *Contemporary Pacific* 3, no. 1 (Spring 1991): 159–167; Jocelyn Linnekin, "Text Bites and the R-Word: The Politics of Representing Scholarship," *Contemporary Pacific* 3, no. 1 (Spring 1991): 172–177.

16. Greg Dening, "History 'in' the Pacific," *Contemporary Pacific: A Journal of Island Affairs* 1, nos. 1 and 2 (Spring and Fall 1989): 134. See also Dening's discussion of how history as a discipline is inscribed in the hegemony of the present in his conclusion to *The Bounty: An Ethnographic History* (Melbourne: History Department, University of Melbourne, 1988). Dening's work on Western penetration of the Marquesas Islands is an outstanding example of how the boundaries between anthropology and history can be breached. See Greg Dening, *Islands and Beaches: Discourse on a Silent Land* (Honolulu: University of Hawaii Press, 1980).

17. Fernand Braudel, *On History*, trans. Sarah Matthews (Chicago: University of Chicago Press, 1980), 74–75. For examples of Braudel's histories, see *Capitalism and Material Life, 1400–1800*, trans. Miriam Kochan (New York: Harper & Row, 1967); and *The Mediterranean and the Mediterranean World in the Age of Philip II*, trans. Sian Reynolds (New York: Harper & Row, 1972).

18. Fredric Jameson, "Marxism and Historicism," *New Literary History* 11 (Autumn 1979): 45. For other Marxist-informed discussions of historiography and ideology, see Fredric Jameson, *The Political Unconscious: Narrative as a Socially Symbolic Act* (Ithaca: Cornell University Press, 1981); Raymond Williams, *The Long Revolution* (New York: Columbia University Press, 1961); and Gregor

McLennan, *Marxism and the Methodologies of History* (London: Verso, 1981), 95–106. McLennan argues that Braudel's views of history and theory are compatible with a flexible Marxist historiography.

19. For discussions that problematize Western historiography and historical narrativity, see the following: Hayden White, "Critical Response: The Narrativization of Real Events," *Critical Inquiry* 7 (Summer 1981): 793–798; Hayden White, "The Value of Narrativity in the Representation of Reality," *Critical Inquiry* 7 (Autumn 1980): 5–27; Peter Brooks, "Fictions of the Wolf Man: Freud and Narrative Understanding," in *Reading for the Plot: Design and Intention in Narrative*, ed. Peter Brooks (New York: Random House, 1985), 264–285; Louis Mink, "Narrative Form as a Cognitive Instrument," in *The Writing of History: Literary Form and Historical Understanding*, ed. Robert H. Canary and Henry Kozicki (Madison: University of Wisconsin Press, 1978), 129–149.

20. Johannes Fabian, *Time and the Other: How Anthropology Makes Its Object* (New York: Columbia University Press, 1983), 143–152. Examples of histories of Hawai'i that start with the arrival of the West are Ralph S. Kuykendall, *The Hawaiian Kingdom*, 3 vols. (Honolulu: University of Hawaii Press, 1938–1967); Lawrence H. Fuchs, *Hawaii Pono: A Social History* (New York: Harcourt, Brace and World, 1961); Gavan Daws, *Shoal of Time: A History of the Hawaiian Islands* (Honolulu: University of Hawaii Press, 1968); Edward Joesting, *Hawaii: An Uncommon History* (New York: Norton, 1972).

21. Borofsky and Howard identify three significant problems in understanding early Polynesian–Western interactions: a predominance of European perspectives, limited theoretical interpretations, and a lack of comparative analysis among island groupings. See Robert Borofsky and Alan Howard, "The Early Contact Period," in *Developments in Polynesian Ethnology*, ed. Alan Howard and Robert Borofsky (Honolulu: University of Hawaii Press, 1989), 241–275.

22. Kenneth Burke, *Counter-Statement* (Berkeley: University of California Press, 1968), 124–125; White, "Value of Narrativity," 27.

23. The fullest account of White's notion of emplotment is found in Hayden White, *Metahistory: The Historical Imagination in Nineteenth-Century Europe* (Baltimore: Johns Hopkins University Press, 1973), 7–11.

24. Noel Kent, *Hawaii: Islands under the Influence* (New York: Monthly Review Press, 1983); David E. Stannard, *Before the Horror: The Population of Hawai'i on the Eve of Western Contact* (Honolulu: Social Science Research Institute, University of Hawaii, 1989); Haunani-Kay Trask, "Hawaiians, American Colonization, and the Quest for Independence," *Social Process in Hawaii* 31 (1984–1985): 101–136.

25. Caroline Ralston, "Hawaii 1778–1854: Some Aspects of Maka'ainana Response to Rapid Cultural Change," *Journal of Pacific History* 19 (1984): 21–40; Edward D. Beechert, *Working in Hawaii: A Labor History* (Honolulu: University of Hawaii Press, 1985); Ronald Takaki, *Pau Hana: Plantation Life and Labor in Hawaii, 1835–1920* (Honolulu: University of Hawaii Press, 1983); Davianna Pomaika'i McGregor, "Kupa'a I Ka 'Aina: Persistence on the Land," Ph.D. dissertation, University of Hawaii, 1989.

26. George Cooper and Gavan Daws, *Land and Power in Hawaii* (Honolulu: Benchmark Books, 1985).

27. Marshall Sahlins, *Historical Metaphors and Mythical Realities: Structure in the Early History of the Sandwich Islands Kingdom* (Ann Arbor: University of Michigan Press, 1981); Marshall Sahlins, *Islands of History* (Chicago: University of Chicago Press, 1985); Jocelyn Linnekin, *Children of the Land: Exchange and Status in a Hawaiian Community* (New Brunswick, N.J.: Rutgers University Press, 1985); Jocelyn Linnekin, *Sacred Queens and Women of Consequence: Rank, Gender, and Colonialism in the Hawaiian Islands* (Ann Arbor: University of Michigan Press, 1990); Valerio Valeri, *Kingship and Sacrifice: Ritual and Sacrifice in Ancient Hawaii*, trans. Paula Wissing (Chicago: University of Chicago Press, 1985); Borofsky and Howard, "Early Contact Period."

28. Examples are Lilikāli Kame'eleihiwa's history of how land moved into foreign hands during the 1800s: Lilikalā Dorton, "Land and the Promise of Capitalism: A Dilemma for the Hawaiian Chiefs of the 1848 *Māhele*," Ph.D. dissertation, University of Hawaii, 1986; and John Charlot, *Chanting the Universe: Hawaiian Religious Culture* (Hong Kong: Emphasis International, 1983).

29. George Marcus, review of *Transformations of Polynesian Culture*, *Pacific Studies* 11, no. 3 (July 1988): 118. For another critique of

the limitations of structural anthropology, see Michael Goldsmith, "Transformations of the Meeting-house in Tuvalu," *Transformations of Polynesian Culture*, ed. Antony Hooper and Judith Huntsman (Auckland, New Zealand: Polynesian Society, 1985), 151–175.

30. Braudel, *On History*, 89.

31. Roland Barthes, "Theory of the Text," in *Untying the Text: A Post-structuralist Reader*, ed. Robert Young (Boston: Routledge and Kegan Paul, 1981), 37–47.

32. Andrew W. Lind, *Hawaii's People*, 3rd ed. (Honolulu: University of Hawaii Press, 1967); Robert C. Schmitt, *Demographic Statistics of Hawaii: 1778–1965* (Honolulu: University of Hawaii Press, 1968); Robert C. Schmitt, *The Missionary Censuses of Hawaii* (Honolulu: Bernice P. Bishop Museum, 1973); Eleanore Nordyke, *The Peopling of Hawaii*, 2nd ed. (Honolulu: University of Hawaii Press, 1989). The estimate of 300,000 at contact is accepted by archaeologist Patrick Kirch, *Feathered Gods and Fishhooks: An Introduction to Hawaiian Archaeology and Prehistory* (Honolulu: University of Hawaii Press, 1985), 286, as the mid-range of varying estimates made by early Western observers. Trask, "Hawaiians, American Colonization, and the Quest for Independence," 110, argues for 500,000, the highest of the estimates made by early observers of Hawai'i. David E. Stannard argues that the estimates of the first explorers seriously underestimated the population. He produces evidence from the fields of archaeology, paleodemography, and geography to argue that the population of Hawai'i was from 800,000 to 1 million. See Stannard, *Before the Horror*. In his review of Stannard's book, Kirch commends Stannard's scholarship and contribution to an issue that is still open for further research. See Patrick Kirch, review of *Before the Horror*, *Contemporary Pacific: A Journal of Island Affairs* 2 of no. 2 (Fall 1990): 394–396.

Chapter Two

1. Fredric Jameson, "Marxism and Historicism," *New Literary History* 11 (Autumn 1979): 41–73.

2. Marx developed his conceptualization of social structure in *Capital* and the major works leading up to it: Karl Marx, *A Contribu-*

tion to the Critique of Political Economy, trans. N. I. Stone (Chicago: Charles H. Kerr, 1904); Karl Marx, *Capital*, 3 vols. (New York: International Publishers, 1967); Karl Marx, *The Grundrisse: Foundations of the Critique of Political Economy*, trans. Martin Nicolaus (New York: Random House, 1973).

3. Louis Althusser, *For Marx*, trans. Ben Brewster (New York: Random House, 1970); Louis Althusser and Etienne Balibar, *Reading Capital*, trans. Ben Brewster (London: New Left Books, 1970). For detailed discussions and critiques of Althusser's theoretical contributions, see the following: Alex Callinicos, *Althusser's Marxism* (London: Pluto Press, 1976); Gregor McLennan, *Marxism and the Methodologies of History* (London: Verso, 1982); Ted Benton, *The Rise and Fall of Structural Marxism: Althusser and His Influence* (London: Macmillan, 1984); Steven B. Smith, *Reading Althusser: An Essay on Structural Marxism* (Ithaca: Cornell University Press, 1984).

4. Althusser, *For Marx*, 111–112, 213, 231–233.

5. Althusser and Balibar, *Reading Capital*, 233–234; Althusser, *For Marx*, 89–116, 209–217.

6. Richard Johnson, "Three Problematics: Elements of a Theory of Working-Class Culture," in *Working Class Culture: Studies in History and Theory*, ed. John Clarke, Chas Critcher, and Richard Johnson (New York: St. Martin's, 1980), 231–232.

7. Antonio Gramsci, *Selections from the Prison Notebooks*, ed. and trans. Quintin Hoare and Geoffrey N. Smith (New York: International Publishers, 1971). Stuart Hall's discussions and applications of Gramsci's notion of hegemony are particularly insightful. See, for instance, Stuart Hall, "The Toad in the Garden," in *Marxism and the Interpretation of Culture*, ed. Cary Nelson and Lawrence Grossberg (Urbana: University of Illinois Press, 1988), 35–73.

8. Althusser, *For Marx*, 89–116, 209–217.

9. In its most extreme formulations, Althusserian structuralism results in histories without subjects or agents. While remaining within the basic structural notion of human action constrained by structure, Giddens argues for a stronger concept of human agency. See Anthony Giddens, *Central Problems in Social Theory: Action, Structure and Contradiction in Social Analysis* (Berkeley: University of California Press, 1979), 141, 131–164; Anthony Giddens, *Social*

Theory and Modern Sociology (Stanford: Stanford University Press, 1987), 86–89. See also Stuart Hall, "Signification, Representation, Ideology: Althusser and the Post-Structuralist Debates," *Critical Studies in Mass Communication* 2 (June 1985): 91–114.

10. For a discussion of the development of French Marxist anthropology, see Maurice Godelier, *Perspectives in Marxist Anthropology* (Cambridge, England: Cambridge University Press, 1977); Joel S. Kahn and Josep R. Llobera, "Towards a New Marxism or a New Anthropology?" in *The Anthropology of Pre-Capitalist Societies*, ed. Joel S. Kahn and Josep R. Llobera (Atlantic Highlands, N.J.: Humanities Press, 1981), 263–329; Maurice Bloch, *Marxism and Anthropology: The History of a Relationship* (Oxford, England: Clarendon Press, 1983).

11. Representative works by these anthropologists include Claude Meillassoux, *Anthropologie Economique des Gouro de Cote d'Ivoire* (Paris-Le Haye: Mouton, 1964); Pierre-Phillippe Rey, *Colonialism, Neo-colonialism, et Transition au Capitalism* (Paris: Maspero, 1971); Maurice Godelier, *Rationality and Irrationality in Economics*, trans. Brian Pearce (New York: Monthly Review Press, 1972); Emmanuel Terray, *Marxism and "Primitive" Societies*, trans. M. Klopper (New York: Monthly Review Press, 1972).

12. Maurice Godelier, "Economy and Religion: An Evolutionary Optical Illusion," in *The Evolution of Social Systems*, ed. J. Friedman and M. J. Rowlands (Pittsburgh: University of Pittsburgh Press, 1978); Maurice Godelier, "Infrastructures, Societies and History," *New Left Review* 112 (November–December 1978); Godelier, *Rationality and Irrationality in Economics*, 95–96.

13. For a succinct discussion of evolving Marxist conceptualizations of culture and ideology and the dialogue between Marxist-informed perspectives with poststructuralism and other cultural studies orientations, see Cary Nelson and Lawrence Grossberg, "Introduction: The Territory of Marxism," in *Marxism and the Interpretation of Culture*, ed. Cary Nelson and Lawrence Grossberg (Urbana: University of Illinois Press, 1988), 1–13.

14. Ferdinand de Saussure, *Course in General Linguistics*, ed. Charles Bally and Albert Sechehaye in collaboration with Albert Reidlinger and trans. Wade Baskin (New York: Philosophical Library,

1959), 120. For a discussion of Saussure's contribution, see Fredric Jameson, *The Prison-House of Language* (Princeton, N.J.: Princeton University Press, 1972), 3–39.

15. Ibid., 140.

16. Ibid., 195; italics added.

17. See the collection of essays in Michael Shapiro, ed., *Language and Politics: Readings in Social and Political Theory* (New York: New York University Press, 1984).

18. For a discussion of how textual interpretation can be related to the historical dimension of changes in modes of production, see Jameson, *Political Unconscious*, 74–102.

19. Jacques Attali, *Noise: The Political Economy of Music*, trans. Brian Massumi (Minneapolis: University of Minnesota Press, 1985).

20. Ibid., 19.

21. Ibid., 34.

Chapter Three

1. The term "tribute-based mode of production" has been used by Marxist anthropologists as a mode-of-production type that roughly encompasses the characteristics of Hawai'i prior to contact. However, "tribute" does not adequately encompass the unique symbolic as well as economic relations between *ali'i* (chiefs) and *maka'āinana* (commoners). I am therefore using the awkward but descriptive term "Hawaiian hierarchical mode of production."

2. For discussions on religious beliefs and practices, see Edward S. Craighill Handy, *Polynesian Religion* (Honolulu: Bishop Museum Press, 1927); Martha W. Beckwith, *Hawaiian Mythology* (Honolulu: University of Hawaii Press, 1970); John Charlot, *Chanting the Universe: Hawaiian Religious Culture* (Hong Kong: Emphasis International, 1983); Valerio Valeri, *Kingship and Sacrifice: Ritual and Society in Ancient Hawaii*, trans. Paula Wissing (Chicago: University of Chicago Press, 1985). For an informative debate between Charlot and Valeri over Hawaiian religious practices and their meanings, see *Pacific Studies* 12, no. 3 (July 1989): 107–147, 148–214.

3. Brad Shore, "*Mana* and *Tapu*," in *Developments in Polynesian*

Ethnology, ed. Alan Howard and Robert Borofsky (Honolulu: University of Hawaii Press, 1989), 137–142.

4. Ibid., 154.

5. Edward S. Craighill Handy, "Cultural Revolution in Hawaii," paper prepared for the Fourth General Session of the Institute of Pacific Relations, Hangchow, China, October 21 to November 4, 1931; reprinted by American Council, Institute of Pacific Relations, 1931, 8; Valeri, *Kingship and Sacrifice*, 155–174.

6. Shore, "*Mana* and *Tapu*," 143–148, 156–165. For a detailed discussion of the ambiguous status of women in Hawai'i, see Jocelyn Linnekin, *Sacred Queens and Women of Consequence: Rank, Gender, and Colonialism in the Hawaiian Islands* (Ann Arbor: University of Michigan Press, 1990).

7. Handy, "Cultural Revolution in Hawaii," 5; Valeri, *Kingship and Sacrifice*, 90–95. *Kauwā* are described in Martha W. Beckwith, ed., *Kepelino's Traditions of Hawaii* (Honolulu: Bernice P. Bishop Museum, 1932), 142–146; David Malo, *Hawaiian Antiquities (Moolele Hawaii)*, 2nd ed., trans. Nathaniel B. Emerson (Honolulu: Bishop Museum Press, 1951), 68–72; Samuel Manaiakalani Kamakau, *Ka Po'e Kahiko: The People of Old*, trans. Mary Kawena Pukui, ed. Dorothy B. Barrère (Honolulu: Bishop Museum Press, 1964), 8–9.

8. Handy, "Cultural Revolution in Hawaii," 14–15.

9. Malo, *Hawaiian Antiquities*, 195.

10. Irving Goldman, *Ancient Polynesian Society* (Chicago: University of Chicago Press, 1970), 10–13; Alan Howard, "Polynesian Social Stratification Revisited: Reflections on Castles Built of Sand (and a Few Bits of Coral)," *American Anthropologist* 74 (August 1972): 811–823; Valeri, *Kingship and Sacrifice*, 95–105.

11. Shore, "*Mana* and *Tapu*," 142–143.

12. Goldman, *Ancient Polynesian Society* (Chicago: University of Chicago Press, 1970), 219.

13. Robert Hommon, "The Formation of Primitive States in Pre-Contact Hawai'i," Ph.D. dissertation, University of Arizona, 1976, 168.

14. Beckwith, *Kepelino's Traditions of Hawaii*, 122–134; Goldman, *Ancient Polynesian Society*, 492–494.

15. Malo, *Hawaiian Antiquities*, 159; Valeri, *Kingship and Sacrifice*, 259.

16. Marshall Sahlins, *Social Stratification in Hawaii* (Seattle: University of Washington Press, 1958); Abraham Fornander, *An Account of the Polynesian Race: Its Origin and Migrations* (Rutland, Vt.: Charles E. Tuttle, 1969), 2:65–66; Goldman, *Ancient Polynesian Society*, 477.

17. One of the classic histories of feudalism is Marc Bloch, *Feudal Society* (Chicago: University of Chicago Press, 1961. See also Perry Anderson's history of feudalism, *Passages from Antiquity to Feudalism* (London: Verso, 1978).

18. Valeri, *Kingship and Sacrifice*, 155. The development and use of the image of Hawai'i as a despotic feudal system by Westerners seeking justification for the imposition of a system of private property and later the overthrow of the monarchy during the 1800s is discussed by Robert H. Stauffer, "Holy Quest: The Puritan Americanization of Hawaii: The Antifeudal Hawaiian Revolution: 1839–1850," Master's thesis, University of Hawaii, 1980.

19. Lilikalā Dorton, "Land and the Promise of Capitalism: A Dilemma for the Hawaiian Chiefs of the 1848 Mahele," Ph.D. dissertation, University of Hawaii, 1986, 23–77.

20. Patrick Vinton Kirch, *The Evolution of the Polynesian Chiefdoms* (Cambridge, England: Cambridge University Press, 1984), 161; Patrick Vinton Kirch, *Feathered Gods and Fishhooks: An Introduction to Hawaiian Archaeology and Prehistory* (Honolulu: University of Hawaii Press, 1985), 216.

21. Handy, "Cultural Revolution," 11; Caroline Ralston, "Hawaii 1778–1854: Some Aspects of Maka'ainana Response to Rapid Cultural Change," *Journal of Pacific History* 19 (1984): 21–40.

22. Malo, *Hawaiian Antiquities*, 142–143. For a structural anthropological account of the *makahiki*, see Valeri, *Kingship and Sacrifice*, 200–233.

23. Jocelyn Linnekin, "Women and Land in Post-Contact Hawaii," paper presented to the Department of Anthropology, University of Hawaii, 1984, 4; Hommon, "The Formation of Primitive States," 75; Kirch, *Feathered Gods and Fishhooks*, 294; Ralston, "Hawaii 1778–1854," 21–40.

24. Dorton, "Land and the Promise of Capitalism," 42.

25. Goldman, *Ancient Polynesian Society*, 12.

26. Martha W. Beckwith, trans. and ed., *The Kumulipo: A Hawaiian Creation Chant* (Honolulu: University Press of Hawaii, 1972), 143; Charlot, *Chanting the Universe*, 21–35; Valerio Valeri, "The Transformation of a Transformation: A Structural Essay on an Aspect of Hawaiian History (1809–1819)," *Social Analysis* 10 (May 1982): 3–41; Valeri, *Kingship and Sacrifice*, 9–36.

27. Valeri, *Kingship and Sacrifice*, 109.

28. Handy, "Cultural Revolution in Hawaii," 11.

29. Malo, *Hawaiian Antiquities*, 71. For descriptions of the priests and their roles, see Kamakau, *Ka Po'e Kahiko*, 7–8; Samuel Manaiakalani Kamakau, *The Works of the People of Old: Na Hana a ka Po'e Kahiko*, trans. Mary Kawena Pukui and ed. Dorothy B. Barrère (Honolulu: Bishop Museum Press, 1976), 30; and Valeri, *Kingship and Sacrifice*, 135–140. Malo's description of the great ritual undertaking involved in the construction of a Kū temple, a *luakini*, shows the nature of rituals led by Kū priests; see Malo, *Hawaiian Antiquities*, 159–176. Valeri, *Kingship and Sacrifice*, 234–338 expands on and interprets the *luakini* temple rituals and the meaning of human sacrifice within Hawaiian cultural categories.

30. Chapter Six is devoted to an analysis of language and power in Hawai'i before and after Western contact.

31. "Ideological apparatus" is a term taken from Althusser's discussion of ideology in "Ideology and Ideological State Apparatuses," in *Lenin and Philosophy and Other Essays* (London: New Left Books, 1971).

32. Apparently, the *maka'āinana* did not maintain their genealogies in a corporate descent model, but were organized through lateral kin relationships, residence and production, and the extended household of *'ohana*. Kirch, *Evolution of the Polynesian Chiefdoms*, 237.

33. Valeri, *Kingship and Sacrifice*, 157.

34. Ibid., 159–161. For the most complete historical account of *ali'i* struggles for power over island territories (including their marriage alliances), see Fornander, *Account of the Polynesian Race*, vol. 2. For an explanation of the structural importance of women in Hawai'i, see Linnekin, *Sacred Queens and Women of Consequence*.

35. Malo, *Hawaiian Antiquities*, 54–56. Only high chiefs, those already sacred, could mate with siblings or other close family members; lower ranking *ali'i* and *maka'āinana* did not do this.

36. Malo, *Hawaiian Antiquities*, 56. See the following for more information on *kapu* and genealogical ranking: Beckwith, *Kepelino's Traditions of Hawaii*, 142; Handy, "Cultural Revolution," 4; Kamakau, *Ka Po'e Kahiko*, 4–5.

37. Goldman, *Ancient Polynesian Society*, 8–9.

38. The most extensive ethnomusicological account of the functions, types, and styles of chant and *hula* is Betty Tatar, *Nineteenth Century Hawaiian Chant* (Honolulu: Bernice P. Bishop Museum, 1982). Tatar has identified more than a hundred Hawaiian terms for designating various types and styles of chants and chanting. See also Nathaniel B. Emerson, *Unwritten Literature of Hawaii: The Sacred Songs of the Hula* (Rutland, Vt.: Charles E. Tuttle, 1965); Dorothy B. Barrère, Mary Kawena Pukui, and Marion Kelly, *Hula: Historical Perspectives* (Honolulu: Bernice Puahi Bishop Museum, 1980).

39. Barrère, Pukui, and Kelly, *Hula*, 212.

40. My analysis of chant and *hula* as expressive forms and social practices is similar to Kaeppler's view of the "arts" as "cultural forms embedded in social action." My stress is on representational forms as ideological and discursive practices. See Adrienne L. Kaeppler, "Art and Aesthetics," in *Developments in Polynesian Ethnography*, ed. Alan Howard and Robert Borofsky (Honolulu: University of Hawaii Press, 1989), 213.

41. Tatar, *Nineteenth Century Hawaiian Chant*, 33.

42. Malo, *Hawaiian Antiquities*, 136.

43. Emerson, *Unwritten Literature of Hawaii*, 13.

44. Cited in Barrère, Pukui, and Kelly, *Hula*, 21.

45. Northrop Frye, *The Great Code: The Bible and Literature* (San Diego: Harcourt Brace Jovanovich, 1982), 32–33.

46. Maurice Bloch, "Symbols, Song, Dance and Features of Articulation: Is Religion an Extreme Form of Traditional Authority?" *European Journal of Sociology* 15 (1974): 55–81.

47. Marshall Sahlins, "Other Times, Other Customs: The Anthropology of History." *American Anthropologist* 85 (1983): 524; Michel Foucault, "The Order of Discourse," in *Language and Politics*, ed.

Michael Shapiro (New York: New York University Press, 1984), 108–138. A number of Hawaiian scholars have discussed the refashioning of genealogical chants to serve immediate political interests, among them, Emerson, *Unwritten Literature of Hawaii*, 116; Beckwith, *Kumulipo*, xviii; Malo, *Hawaiian Antiquities*, 71; John Charlot, *The Hawaiian Poetry of Religion and Politics: Some Religio-Political Concepts in Postcontact Literature* (Honolulu: Brigham Young University–Hawaii Campus, 1985), 4.

48. Beckwith, *Kumulipo*, 1–4. The first English translation of the Kalākaua text of the chant was done by Queen Lili'uokalani after the overthrow while she was in detention at Washington Place in Honolulu: *An Account of the World According to Hawaiian Tradition* (Boston: Lee and Shepard, 1897).

49. Howard, "Polynesian Social Stratification Revisited," 822; Goldman, *Ancient Polynesian Society*, 481.

50. See Anthony Giddens's discussion of precapitalist, class-divided societies in his *A Contemporary Critique of Historical Materialism: Power, Property and the State* (Berkeley: University of California Press, 1983), 105–108.

51. Malo, *Hawaiian Antiquities*, 6; Charlot, *Chanting the Universe*, 146–147; Fornander, *Account of the Polynesian Race*, 2:33–38, 58–62; Peter H. Buck, *Vikings of the Pacific* (Chicago: University of Chicago Press, 1938), 257–266.

52. Malo, *Hawaiian Antiquities*, 56; Kamakau, *Ka Po'e Kahiko*, 12; Beckwith, *Kumulipo*, 17.

53. Hommon, "The Formation of Primitive States," 229–231; Ross H. Cordy, "Cultural Adaptation and Evolution in Hawaii: A Suggested New Sequence," *Journal of the Polynesian Society* 83 (1974): 180–191; Ross H. Cordy, *A Study of Prehistorical Social Change: The Development of Complex Societies in the Hawaiian Islands* (New York: Academic Press, 1981); Kirch, *Feathered Gods and Fishhooks*, 298–308. For a critique of Kirch's reconstruction of pre-Western contact Hawai'i, see David E. Stannard, *Before the Horror: The Population of Hawai'i on the Eve of Western Contact* (Honolulu: Social Science Research Institute, University of Hawaii, 1989).

54. For a general discussion of the notion of "occupying" and "transforming" economies in the transformative processes, see Mau-

rice Godelier, *Rationality and Irrationality in Economics*, trans. Brian Pearce (New York: Monthly Review Press, 1972), 263–277.

55. Charlot, *Chanting the Universe*, 144–148. See also Charlot's discussion of changes in the chants and stories of Kamapua'a as part of social and political changes, in John Charlot, *The Kamapua'a Literature: The Classical Traditions of the Hawaiian Pig God as a Body of Literature*, Monograph Series No. 6 (La'ie, Hawai'i: Institute for Polynesian Studies, Brigham Young University–Hawai'i Campus, 1987).

56. For a discussion of the emergence of class division as part of the development of state formations in Tonga prior to Western contact, see Christine W. Gailey, *Kinship to Kingship: Gender Hierarchy and State Formation in the Tongan Islands*, Sourcebooks in Anthropology no. 14 (Austin: University of Texas Press, 1987). A distinction can be made between class formation and class consciousness. It can be argued that in Hawai'i what Marxist theory conceptualizes as class consciousness did not appear until after Western contact and particularly the sandalwood trading period in which there was heavy exploitation of *maka'āinana* by *ali'i*.

57. Fornander, *Account of the Polynesian Race*, 2:63.

58. Kirch, *Feathered Gods and Fishhooks*, 235. The Marshall Sahlins citation in the quote is from *Stone Age Economics* (Chicago: Aldine-Atherton, 1972).

59. Sahlins, *Stone Age Economics*, 144.

60. Kirch, *Evolution of Polynesian Chiefdoms*, 201–207; Valeri, *Kingship and Sacrifice*, 160–161.

61. Malo, *Hawaiian Antiquities*, 58, 195.

62. Kirch, *Evolution of Polynesian Chiefdoms*, 257.

63. Maurice Godelier, "Infrastructures, Societies and History," *New Left Review* 112 (1978): 84–96.

64. Maurice Bloch, "The Past and the Present in the Present," *Man* 12 (1977): 289.

65. Goldman, *Ancient Polynesian Society*, xviii.

66. Ralston, "Hawaii 1778–1854," 22. Hommon also notes that demands for goods by the chiefly system rarely led to hardship on the *maka'āinana*, although warfare frequently involved raids against and destruction of agricultural fields: Hommon, "Formation of Primitive States," 281–284. And Stannard, in refuting Kirch's argument that

the islands had reached their capacity to support the population, cites numerous descriptions from early explorers of healthy, robust and active people with plentiful supplies of food. Stannard, *Before the Horror*, 66–69.

67. Marshall Sahlins, *Islands of History* (Chicago: University of Chicago Press, 1985), 20.

Chapter Four

1. See Eric Wolf, *Europe and the People without History* (Berkeley: University of California Press, 1982).

2. Marc Bloch, *Feudal Society* (Chicago: University of Chicago Press, 1961); Perry Anderson, *Passages from Antiquity to Feudalism* (London: Verso, 1978).

3. Aidan Foster-Carter, "The Modes of Production Controversy," *New Left Review* 107 (January/February 1978): 1–31.

4. Alan Trachtenburg, *The Incorporation of America: Culture and Society in the Gilded Age* (New York: Hill and Wang, 1982), 11–37.

5. For descriptions of this period, see Theodore Morgan, *A Century of Economic Change* (Cambridge, Mass.: Harvard University Press, 1948); Abraham Fornander, *An Account of the Polynesian Race: Its Origin and Migrations, and the Ancient History of the Hawaiian People to the Times of Kamehameha I* (Rutland, Vt.: Charles E. Tuttle, 1965), 2: 200–349; Harold Whitman Bradley, *The American Frontier in Hawaii: The Pioneers, 1789–1843* (Gloucester, Mass.: Peter Smith, 1968), 13–54, 222–223; Noel Kent, *Hawaii: Islands under the Influence* (New York: Monthly Review Press, 1983), 11–14. For a discussion of Western trade and extraction of resources throughout the Pacific during the eighteenth and nineteenth centuries, including Hawai'i, see Caroline Ralston, *Grass Huts and Warehouses: Pacific Beach Communities of the Nineteenth Century* (Honolulu: University Press of Hawaii, 1978).

6. Valerio Valeri, "The Transformation of a Transformation: A Structural Essay on an Aspect of Hawaiian History (1809–1819)," *Social Analysis* 10 (May 1982): 30–31. Kaeppler provides a different assessment of the results of Kamehameha's actions (a down-

playing of genealogical descent and the elevation of the war god Kūkā'ilimoku, which changed the locus of power), although she agrees that a major transformation did occur from Kamehameha's actions. See Adrienne L. Kaeppler, "Hawaiian Art and Society: Traditions and Transformations," in *Transformations of Polynesian Culture*, ed. Antony Hooper and Judith Huntsman (Auckland, New Zealand: Polynesian Society, 1985), 105–108. Dorton's analysis of land and power shows how Kamehameha I's change in land tenure—giving certain *ali'i* rights in perpetuity to their land, which Ka'ahumanu extended to all *ali'i* after Kamehameha's death—undercut the power of later kings vis-à-vis the *ali'i* and Westerners. See Lilikalā Dorton, "Land and the Promise of Capitalism: A Dilemma for the Hawaiian Chiefs of the 1848 Mahele," Ph.D. dissertation, University of Hawaii, 1986, 80–90.

7. Marshall Sahlins, *Islands of History* (Chicago: University of Chicago Press, 1985), 77.

8. Sahlins argues that Cook, coming during the period of the Makahiki, was perceived by Hawaiians as the god Lono. Marshall Sahlins, *Historical Metaphors and Mythical Realities: Structure in the Early History of the Sandwich Islands Kingdom* (Ann Arbor: University of Michigan Press, 1981), 17–28. Obeyesekere claims this is a Western myth and a Eurocentric perception of Hawaiians. Gananath Obeyesekere, *The Apotheosis of Captain Cook: European Mythmaking in the Pacific* (Princeton: Princeton University Press, 1992).

9. Jocelyn Linnekin, "Inside, Outside: A Hawaiian Community in the World System," Department of Anthropology, University of Hawaii at Manoa, 1985, 42–53, photocopy; Sahlins, *Islands of History*, 138.

10. Brad Shore, "*Mana* and *Tapu*," in *Developments in Polynesian Ethnology*, ed. Alan Howard and Robert Borofsky (Honolulu: University of Hawaii Press, 1989), 165.

11. Caroline Ralston, "Hawaii 1778–1854: Some Aspects of the Maka'ainana Response to Rapid Cultural Change," *Journal of Pacific History* 19 (1984): 32.

12. Sahlins, *Islands of History*, 143.

13. Louis Althusser, *For Marx*, trans. Ben Brewster (New York: Random House, 1970), 99, 89–116, 209–217.

14. For descriptions of the sandalwood trade and its economic and political implications, see Kent, *Hawaii*, 17–21; Ralph Kuykendal, *The Hawaiian Kingdom* (Honolulu: University of Hawaii Press, 1938), 1:85–92; Bradley, *American Frontier in Hawaii*, 53–120, 6–68, 106–114.

15. Valeri, "Transformation of a Transformation," 32. For an account of Kamehameha's battles of conquest, his strategy of unification, and the role played by foreigners, particularly Captain Vancouver, in these internal struggles, see Fornander, *Account of the Polynesian Race*, 2:299–349.

16. Sahlins, *Islands of History*, 138–140.

17. Analyses of African structural transformations during the slave trade period by Marxist structural anthropologists are relevant to understanding the economic relationships between *ali'i* and Western traders during the sandalwood period in Hawai'i. See Georges Dupre and Pierre-Philippe Rey, "Reflections on the Pertinence of a Theory of the History of Exchange," *Economy and Society* 2 (1973): 131–163. See also Foster-Carter, "Modes of Production Controversy," 13–16. For further discussion of Hawaiian responses to the penetration of capitalism, see Jocelyn Linnekin, *Sacred Queens and Women of Consequence: Rank, Gender, and Colonialism in the Hawaiian Islands* (Ann Arbor: University of Michigan Press, 1990).

18. For examples of statements about the personal shortcomings of the *ali'i*, see K. R. Howe, *Where the Waves Fall: A New South Sea Islands History from First Settlement to Colonial Rule* (Honolulu: University of Hawaii Press, 1984), 160–169; Fornander, *Account of the Polynesian Race*, 2:246; Kent, *Hawaii*, 22.

19. Robert Borofsky and Alan Howard, "The Early Contact Period," in *Developments in Polynesian Ethnography*, ed. Alan Howard and Robert Borofsky (Honolulu: University of Hawaii Press, 1989), 241–275.

20. Maurice Godelier, *Rationality and Irrationality in Economics*, trans. Brian Pearce (New York: Monthly Review Press, 1972), 99. See Ralston, "Hawaii 1778–1854," 36–37, for a discussion of the hold of the Hawaiian hierarchical ideology on the *maka'āinana* after contact.

21. Kent, *Hawaii*, 21–25; Bradley, *American Frontier in Hawaii*, 79–82, 215–219.

22. Linnekin, "Inside, Outside," 16.

23. Kuykendall, *Hawaiian Kingdom*, 271.

24. For an account of this first sugar plantation, see Ronald Takaki, *Pau Hana: Plantation Life and Labor in Hawaii, 1835–1920* (Honolulu: University of Hawaii Press, 1983), 3–21.

25. *The Friend*, August 1845, 118.

26. Judge Lee's statement was quoted in an article by W. D. Alexander, "Early Industrial Teaching of Hawaiians," in *Hawaiian Almanac and Annual for 1895*, ed. and comp. Thomas G. Thrum (Honolulu, 1894), 97–98.

27. Robert Schmitt, *Demographic Statistics of Hawaii: 1778–1965* (Honolulu: University of Hawaii Press, 1968), 37.

28. Linnekin, "Women and Land," 6.

29. The term "Great *Māhele*" is applied to the period of land division between 1846 and 1855. For information on the results, see Marion A. Kelly, "Land Tenure in Hawaii," *Amerasia Journal* 7 (1980): 57–73; Haunani-Kay Trask, "Hawaiians, American Colonization, and the Quest for Independence," *Social Process in Hawaii* 31 (1984–1985), 110–112; Lilikalā Dorton, "Land and the Promise of Capitalism"; Kent, *Hawaii*, 31–35; Bradley, *American Frontier in Hawaii*, 277–282; Linnekin, *Sacred Queens and Women of Consequence*; Kuykendall, *Hawaiian Kingdom*, 1:269–298.

30. Amos Starr Cooke, *The Chiefs' Children's School, a Record Compiled from the Diary and Letters of Amos Starr Cooke and Juliette Montague Cooke, by Their Granddaughter Mary Atherton Richards* (Honolulu: Printed by the *Honolulu Star-Bulletin* 1937), 349–350, in Dorton, "Land and the Promise of Capitalism," 321.

31. Linnekin, "Inside, Outside," 20.

32. See Jocelyn Linnekin, *Children of the Land: Exchange and Status in a Hawaiian Community* (New Brunswick, N.J.: Rutgers University Press, 1985), for an account of how one predominantly Hawaiian community on Maui integrated the communal system with capitalism. See also Alan Howard, *Ain't No Big Thing: Coping Strategies in a Hawaiian-American Community* (Honolulu: University of Hawaii Press, 1974), for a discussion of the surviving communal values among Hawaiians living along the Wai'anae coast of O'ahu.

33. James A. Geschwender, "The Interplay between Class and National Consciousness in Hawaii, 1850–1950," State University of New York at Binghamton, n.d., 19, photocopy.

34. For descriptions and analyses of the plantation system, the conditions of the workers, and the rise of unions in Hawai'i, see Takaki, *Pau Hana*, 127–164. Also see Edward D. Beechert, "The Political Economy of Hawaii and Working Class Consciousness," *Social Process in Hawaii* 31 (1984–1985): 155–181; Edward D. Beechert, *Working in Hawaii: A Labor History* (Honolulu: University of Hawaii Press, 1985).

35. Thomas G. Thrum, ed. and comp., *Hawaiian Almanac and Annual* (Honolulu, 1875–1932).

36. Kuykendall, *Hawaiian Kingdom*, 3:523–534; Queen Liliuo'kalani, *Hawaii's Story by Hawaii's Queen* (Tokyo: Charles E. Tuttle, 1964); Davianna McGregor-Alegado, "Hawaiian Resistance 1887–1889," master's thesis, University of Hawaii, 1979.

37. Ralston, "Hawai'i 1778–1854," 38.

Chapter Five

1. The following discussions draw on a number of scholars concerned with the relationship between history, social structure, and social representation, including the following: Terry Eagleton, *Marxism and Literary Criticism* (Berkeley: University of California Press, 1976); Norman Bryson, *Vision and Painting: The Logic of the Gaze* (New Haven: Yale University Press, 1983); Raymond Williams, *Marxism and Literature* (Oxford, England: Oxford University Press, 1977); Raymond Williams, *The Long Revolution* (New York: Columbia University Press, 1961); Fredric Jameson, *The Political Unconscious: Narrative as a Socially Symbolic Act* (Ithaca: Cornell University Press, 1981); Cary Nelson and Lawrence Grossberg, eds., *Marxism and the Interpretation of Culture* (Urbana, Illinois: University of Illinois Press, 1988). For a perceptive analysis of the social transformation of Hawai'i and manifestations of this transformation in Hawaiian artifacts and works of art, specifically Hawaiian feather cloaks and capes, see Adrienne Kaeppler, "Hawaiian Art and Society:

Traditions and Transformations," in *Transformations of Polynesian Culture*, ed. Antony Hooper and Judith Huntsman (Auckland, New Zealand: Polynesian Society, 1985), 105–131.

2. Kirch argues that variations within the Hawaiian archipelago have been largely ignored by anthropologists and historians. He cites differences in styles of fishhooks, *poi* pounders, sculpture, etc., speculating that such differences may have to do with class distinctions, survival of older traditions, local creativity, or all three. See Patrick Kirch, "Regional Variation and Local Style: A Neglected dimension in Hawaiian Prehistory," *Pacific Studies* 13, no. 2 (1990): 41–54. Still, such variations do not contradict the existence of a coherent Hawaiian culture prior to contact.

3. Roger Wallis and Krister Malm, *Big Sounds from Small People: The Music Industry in Small Countries* (London: Constable, 1984); Elizabeth Bentzel Buck, "The Hawaii Music Industry," *Social Process in Hawaii* 31 (1984–1985): 141–142.

4. I am using the word "culture" in a restricted sense to refer to accessible forms, products, and practices of social representation, including literature, music, art, dance, and various kinds of popular culture production. As John Charlot has pointed out, Hawaiian-language sources such as the Hawaiian language newspapers flourished from the mid-1800s to the end of the century. In addition, Hawaiian writers of the nineteenth century wrote chants, other styles of poetry, music, and literature, much of which have not been translated into English.

5. Edward Joesting, *Hawaii: An Uncommon History* (New York: Norton, 1972), 156–157. Thomas G. Thrum, ed. and comp., *Hawaiian Almanac and Annual* (Honolulu, 1875–1932), are good sources of informal Western-oriented information on Hawai'i.

6. Edward B. Scott, *The Saga of the Sandwich Islands*, vol. 1 (Lake Tahoe, Nevada: Sierra–Tahoe Publishing, 1968), 150. Margaret Mary Frowe, "The History of the Theatre during the Reign of King Kalakaua, 1874–1891," master's thesis, University of Hawaii, 1937; George S. Kanahele, *Hawaiian Music and Musicians: An Illustrated History* (Honolulu: University Press of Hawaii, 1979), 203.

7. Alan Trachtenburg, *The Incorporation of America: Culture and Society in the Gilded Age* (New York: Hill and Wang, 1982), 71.

8. Jacques Attali, *Noise: The Political Economy of Music*, trans. Brian Massumi (Minneapolis: University of Minnesota Press, 1985), 32.

9. Mazeppa King Costa, "Dance in the Society and Hawaiian Islands as Presented by Early Writers, 1767–1842," master's thesis, University of Hawaii, 1951), 62.

10. Otto von Kotzebue, *A New Voyage Round the World in the Years 1823–1826* (Amsterdam, Netherlands: N. Israel, 1967), 2:254–257.

11. Caroline Ralston, "Early Nineteenth Century Polynesian Millennial Cults and the Case of Hawai'i," *Journal of the Polynesian Society* 94 (December 1985): 314–318. For a Hawaiian insider's perspective on the political tensions during this period, see John Papa Īi, *Fragments of Hawaiian History*, trans. Mary Kawena Pukui and ed. Dorothy B. Barrère (Honolulu: Bishop Museum Press, 1959), 141–160.

12. Charles Wilkes, the commander of the 1842 U.S. Exploring Expedition, noted that evening assemblies by Hawaiians were discouraged, their amusements "punished by severe penalties." Cited in Costa, "Dance in the Society and Hawaiian Islands," 128.

13. Thrum, *Hawaiian Almanac and Annual for 1884* (Honolulu, 1885), 65.

14. Adrienne L. Kaeppler, "Dance and the Interpretation of Pacific Traditional Literature," in *Directions in Pacific Traditional Literature: Essays in Honor of Katharine Luomala*, ed. Adrienne L. Kaeppler and H. Arlo Nimmo (Honolulu: Bishop Museum Press, 1976), 195–216. Tatar points out that there was no equivalent Hawaiian word for "music." See Elizabeth Tatar, *Nineteenth Century Hawaiian Chant* (Honolulu: Bernice P. Bishop Museum, 1982), 23.

15. Kaeppler, "Dance," 210.

16. Gilles Deleuze and Felix Guattari introduce this concept in *Anti-Oedipus: Capitalism and Schizophrenia*, trans. Robert Hurley, Mark Seem, and Helen R. Lane (New York: Viking, 1977). For a discussion in the context of Marxist literary theory, see Fredric Jameson, "Beyond the Cave: Modernism and Modes of Production," in *The Horizon of Literature*, ed. Paul Hernadi (Lincoln: University of Nebraska Press, 1982), 172–173.

17. John E. Reinecke, *Language and Dialect in Hawaii: A Sociolinguistic History to 1935*, ed. Stanley M. Tsuzaki (Honolulu: University of Hawaii Press, 1969), 104.

18. Tatar, *Nineteenth Century Hawaiian Chant*, 28; Reinecke, *Language and Dialect*, 29, 37; John Charlot, "William Charles Lunalilo's *'Alekoki* as an Example of Cultural Synthesis in 19th Century Hawaiian Literature," *Journal of the Polynesian Society* 91 (September 1982): 435–444. The last Hawaiian-language newspaper ceased publication in 1948 in Hilo. The number of Hawaiian-language newspapers increased during the later part of the 1880s, peaking in 1896 with fourteen newspapers, this large number reflecting the intense political debates generated over loss of Hawaiian sovereignty in 1893 and Home Rule in the two decades or so after. As the Home Rule movement waned, so did Hawaiian-language newspapers, decreasing to twelve in 1910, eight in 1920, and three in 1930. See Esther K. Mookini, *The Hawaiian Newspapers* (Honolulu: Topgallant Publishing, 1974).

19. John Charlot, *The Hawaiian Poetry of Religion and Politics: Some Religio-Political Concepts in Postcontact Literature* (Honolulu: Institute for Polynesian Studies, Brigham Young University–Hawaii Campus, 1985), 9–14. See also Amy Ku'uleialoha Stillman, "*The Hula Ku'i*: A Tradition in Hawaiian Music and Dance," master's thesis, University of Hawaii, 1982, 16.

20. Kaeppler, "Dance," 214.

21. A. Marques, "Ancient Hawaiian Music," in Thrum, *Hawaiian Almanac and Annual for 1914* (Honolulu, 1915), 97–107.

22. Ibid., 97.

23. Elizabeth Tatar, "Chant," in *Hawaiian Music and Musicians: An Illustrated History*, ed. George S. Kanahele (Honolulu: University of Hawaii Press, 1979), 67.

24. See Tatar, *Nineteenth Century Hawaiian Chant*, 1–14, for a discussion of the research difficulties faced by twentieth-century scholars of chant, as well as the limited availability of sources, published and unpublished, on chant.

25. Kaeppler, "Dance," 201.

26. Amy Stillman, "History Reinterpreted in Song: The Case of the Hawaiian Counterrevolution," *Hawaiian Journal of History* 23 (1989): 1–30, 23.

27. For detailed explanations of late-nineteenth-century changes in *hula*, see Tatar, *Nineteenth Century Hawaiian Chant*, 26–30, 109–115; Elizabeth Tatar, *Strains of Change: The Impact of Tourism on Hawaiian Music*, Special Publication No. 78 (Honolulu: Bernice P. Bishop Museum, 1987); Stillman, "*Hula Kuʻi*," 152–156; Stillman, "History Reinterpreted," 19–25.

28. *Na Himeni Haipule Hawaii*, Sesquicentennial ed. (Honolulu: Hawaii Conference United Church of Christ, 1972): xii–xiv.

29. Tatar, *Nineteenth Century Hawaiian Chant*, 28–29.

30. Kanahele, *Hawaiian Music and Musicians*, 2. See Samuel H. Elbert and Noelani Mahoe, comps., *Na Mele o Hawaiʻi Nei: 101 Hawaiian Songs* (Honolulu: University of Hawaii Press, 1970), for examples of Hawaiian songs composed between 1850 and 1968.

31. Kanahele, *Hawaiian Music and Musicians*, 200–203, 224–232.

32. Ibid., 34–44, 335–344.

33. From *Na Mele O Hawaiʻi Nei*, collected by Samuel H. Elbert and Noelani Mahoe (Honolulu: University of Hawaii Press, 1970), 62–64. See Stillman, "History Reinterpreted in Song," for a discussion on this and other protest songs during the period of the overthrow and annexation.

34. Charlot, *Hawaiian Poetry*, 15.

35. Eleanor Williamson, "Hawaiian Chants and Songs Used in Political Campaigns," in Kaeppler and Nimmo, *Directions in Pacific Traditional Literature*, 137–138.

36. Charlot, *Hawaiian Poetry* 22–23.

37. A language-immersion program, *Aha Punana Leo*, that started with preschoolers, has now moved into elementary schools in a few island communities. This is a concerted effort to revive the Hawaiian language that has received state support.

38. Jameson, *Political Unconscious*, 95–102.

Chapter Six

1. Raymond Williams, *Marxism and Literature* (Oxford, England: Oxford University Press, 1977), 21–44.

2. Walter J. Ong, *Orality and Literacy: The Technologizing of the Word* (London: Methuen, 1982), 85. See also Jack Goody, *The*

Domestication of the Savage Mind (Cambridge, England: Cambridge University Press, 1977).

3. Ong, *Orality and Literacy*, 12, makes this point citing Homeric poetry.

4. John Charlot, *Chanting the Universe: Hawaiian Religious Culture* (Hong Kong: Emphasis International, 1983), 55–78; Martha W. Beckwith, ed., *The Kumulipo: A Hawaiian Creation Chant* (Honolulu: University Press of Hawaii, 1972), 71.

5. Nathaniel B. Emerson, *Unwritten Literature of Hawaii: The Sacred Songs of the Hula* (Rutland, Vt.: Charles E. Tuttle, 1965), 26–27.

6. David Malo, *Hawaiian Antiquities (Moolelo Hawaii)*, trans. Nathaniel B. Emerson, 2nd ed. (Honolulu: Bishop Museum Press, 1951), 191–192.

7. Elizabeth Tatar, "Chant," in *Hawaiian Music and Musicians: An Illustrated History*, ed. George S. Kanahele (Honolulu: University Press of Hawaii, 1979), 53.

8. Mary Kawena Pukui, E. W. Haertig, and Catherine A. Lee, *Nānā I Ke Kumu* (Look to the Source), vol. 1 (Honolulu: Queen Lili'uokalani Children's Center, 1972), 86.

9. Beckwith, *The Kumulipo*, 7–11, 40–41.

10. Ralph Kuykendall, *The Hawaiian Kingdom* (Honolulu: University of Hawaii Press, 1938), 1:104.

11. Ong, *Orality and Literacy*, 52–54.

12. John F. Pogue, *Moolelo of Ancient Hawaii*, trans. Charles W. Kenn (Honolulu: Topgallant Publishing, 1978), 140–141.

13. C. M. Hyde, "The Educational Work of the American Mission for the Hawaiian People," in *Hawaiian Almanac and Annual for 1891*, ed. and comp. Thomas G. Thrum (Honolulu, 1892), 119–120.

14. Michel Foucault, *The History of Sexuality: An Introduction*, trans. Robert Hurley (New York: Random House, 1980), 1:131.

15. Vincent Descombes, *Modern French Philosophy*, trans. L. Scott-Fox and J. M. Harding (Cambridge, England: Cambridge University Press, 1980), 106.

16. To the extent that historians such as Kuykendall talk about the change in language, it is usually in the context of education and the introduction of English-language schools.

17. Ferdinand de Saussure, *Course in General Linguistics*, ed. Charles Bally and Albert Sechehaye in collaboration with Albert Reidlinger and trans. Wade Baskin (New York: Philosophical Library, 1959), 195. See Chapter Two for a fuller discussion of Saussure on language change.

18. Tracy B. Strong, "Language and Nihilism: Nietzsche's Critique of Epistemology," in *Language and Politics*, ed. Michael Shapiro (New York: New York University Press, 1984), 91. See also Michel Foucault, "Nietzsche, Genealogy, History," in *Language, Counter-Memory, Practice: Selected Essays*, ed. and trans. D. R. Bouchard (Ithaca: Cornell University Press, 1977).

19. Strong, "Language and Nihilism," 99.

20. Antonio Gramsci, *Selections from the Prison Notebooks*, ed. and trans. Quintin Hoare and Geoffrey Nowell Smith (New York: International Publishers, 1971), 451–452. Gramsci's discussion of the hegemony of one national language over another as part of social transformation is relevant to Hawai'i's linguistic history.

21. The most perceptive sociological study on the social aspects of the linguistic transformations of Hawai'i was written by John Reinecke in the early 1930s, later edited and reissued. See John E. Reinecke, *Language and Dialect in Hawaii: A Sociolinguistic History to 1935*, ed. Stanley M. Tsuzaki (Honolulu: University of Hawaii Press, 1969), 33.

22. Richard Armstrong, minister of education from 1847 to 1860, *Report* of 1858, cited in Reinecke, *Language and Dialect*, 45.

23. C. M. Hyde, "Educational Work of the American Mission," 120.

24. Esther K. Mookini, *The Hawaiian Newspapers* (Honolulu: Topgallant Publishing, 1974).

25. Reinecke, *Language and Dialect*, 141.

26. *Hawaiian Phrase Book (Na Huaolelo, a me na Olelo Kikeke, ma ka Olelo Beretania a me ka Olelo Hawaii)* (Rutland, Vt.: Charles E. Tuttle, 1968).

27. Michel Foucault, "The Order of Discourse," in *Language and Politics*, ed. Michael Shapiro (New York: New York University Press, 1984), 108–138.

28. See Adrienne L. Kaeppler, "Dance and the Interpretation of Pacific Traditional Literature," in *Directions in Pacific Traditional*

Literature, ed. Adrienne L. Kaeppler and H. Arlo Nimmo (Honolulu: Bishop Museum Press, 1976), for a description of Hawaiian attentiveness in contrast to Asian inattentiveness at performances where dance is used to dramatize narratives from a *written* tradition.

29. Charlot, *Chanting the Universe,* 120.

30. Nathaniel Emerson, in Malo, *Hawaiian Antiquities,* 139–140.

31. Foucault, "Order of Discourse," 112.

32. Ibid., 121–122.

33. Ong, *Orality and Literacy,* 32–77, 146; Goody, *Domestication of the Savage Mind,* 25–27. See John Charlot, "The Application of Form and Redaction Criticism to Hawaiian Literature," *Journal of the Polynesian Society* 86 (1977): 479–501, for a detailed discussion of Hawaiian chant and the processes of composition.

34. Tzvetan Todorov, *The Conquest of America: The Question of the Other,* trans. Richard Howard (New York: Harper & Row, 1984), 3–50, 168–182.

35. George Dixon, *A Voyage Round the World: But More Particularly to the North-West Coast of America: Performed in 1785, 1786, 1787, and 1788* (London: Geo. Goulding, 1789).

36. Loren Eiseley, *Darwin's Century: Evolution and the Men Who Discovered It,* (Garden City, N.Y.: Doubleday, 1961), 18.

37. Michel Foucault, *The Order of Things: An Archaeology of the Human Sciences* (New York: New York University Press, 1984), 134.

38. Cited in Eiseley, *Darwin's Century,* 22.

39. Foucault, *Order of Things,* 309.

40. Todorov, *Conquest of America,* 240.

41. Foucault, *Order of Things,* 312.

42. William Ellis. *An Authentic Narrative of a Voyage Performed by Captain Cook and Captain Clerke, in His Majesty's Ships Resolution and Discovery. During the Years 1776, 1777, 1778, 1779 and 1780 in Search of a North-West-Passage between the Continents of Asia and America,* 3rd ed. (London, 1784), 2:149, 150, 153.

43. Ibid., 169–171.

44. Bernard Smith, *European Vision and the South Pacific, 1768–1850: A Study in the History of Art and Ideas* (London: Oxford University Press, 1960). Smith's book is a fascinating account of how artists, working in a period intersected by neoclassical romanticism and

eighteenth-century notions of nature, pictured people of the Pacific. For the complete collection of artists' drawings, paintings, and engraving from Cook's voyages, see Rüdiger Joppien and Bernard Smith, *The Art of Captain Cook's Voyages* (New Haven: Yale University Press, 1985).

45. Dixon, *Voyage Round the World*, 277–278.

46. Kuykendall, *Hawaiian Kingdom*, 21. For a discussion of Vancouver's actions and intentions regarding relationships between Britain and Hawai'i and Vancouver's attempts to influence Kamehameha and other Hawaiian chiefs, see Marion Kelly, "Some Problems with Early Descriptions of Hawaiian Culture," in *Polynesian Culture and History: Essays in Honor of Kenneth P. Emory*, ed. Genevieve A. Highland, Roland W. Force, Alan Howard, Marion Kelly, and Yoshihiko H. Sinoto (Honolulu: Bishop Museum Press, 1967).

47. George Vancouver, *A Voyage of Discovery to the North Pacific Ocean and Round the World, 1791–1795*, ed. W. Kaye Lamb (London: Hakluyt Society, 1984), 1172.

48. Ibid., 1173.

49. Ibid., 883.

50. Adelbert von Chamisso, "Chamisso in Hawaii," from Chamisso's *Account of the Voyage Around the World on the Rurik, 1815–1818*, trans. Victor S. K. Houston, in Forty-Eighth Annual Report of the Hawaiian Historical Society (Honolulu, 1940), 68.

51. Ibid., 64.

52. Ibid., 69.

53. Hiram Bingham, *A Residence of Twenty-One Years in the Sandwich Islands, or the Civil, Religious, and Political History of Those Islands* (Rutland, Vt.: Charles E. Tuttle, 1981), 23.

54. Ibid., 17.

55. Ibid., 96, 60–61.

56. James Axtell, *The European and the Indian: Essays in the Ethnohistory of Colonial North America* (Oxford, England: Oxford University Press, 1981), 49. For instance, in the 1830s under the terms of the Removal Act, the U.S. government during Andrew Jackson's administration was forceably removing Cherokee Indians and all other Indians remaining in the Southeast to western reservations in Oklahoma. In the 1890s, American forces were still trying to subdue the

Hopi in the Southwest. Peter Matthiessen, *Indian Country* (New York: Penguin Books, 1984).

57. W. Lloyd Warner, *The Family of God: A Symbolic Study of Christian Life in America* (New Haven: Yale University Press, 1961), 137.

58. William Ellis, *Polynesian Researches: Hawaii* (Rutland, Vt.: Charles E. Tuttle, 1969), 2.

59. Sandra E. Wagner, "Mission and Motivation: The Theology of the Early American Mission in Hawai'i," *Hawaiian Journal of History* 19 (1985): 65.

60. Ibid., 62–70; Bingham, *Residence of Twenty-One Years*, 214, 277.

61. Cited in Kuykendall, *Hawaiian Kingdom*, 116.

62. Patricia Grimshaw, "New England Missionary Wives, Hawaiian Women, and 'The Cult of True Womanhood,' " *Hawaiian Journal of History* 19 (1985): 75.

63. William Richards, "William Richards' Report to the Sandwich Islands Mission on His First Year in Government Service, 1838–1839," in Annual Report of the Hawaiian Historical Society for the Year 1943 (Honolulu, 1944), 66. *Pono* means "righteous."

64. Philip Greven, *The Protestant Temperament: Patterns of Child-Rearing, Religious Experience, and the Self in Early America* (New York: New American Library, 1977), 14.

65. Warner, *Family of God*, 62.

66. Grimshaw, "New England Missionary Wives," 81.

67. Bingham, *Residence of Twenty-One Years*, 123–125.

68. Ibid., 129.

69. Alan Trachtenberg, *The Incorporation of America: Culture and Society in the Gilded Age* (New York: Hill and Wang, 1982), 140–161.

70. Joseph Kerman, *Contemplating Music: Challenges to Musicology* (Cambridge, Mass.: Harvard University Press, 1985), 11–30.

71. Ibid., 64–75.

72. Foucault, "Order of Discourse," 118–119, 120.

73. For discussions of ethnomusicology, its development, and issues in the field, see John Shepherd, Phil Virden, Graham Vulliamy and Trevor Wishart, eds., *Whose Music? A Sociology of Musical Lan-*

guages (New Brunswick, N.J.: Transaction Books, 1977); Bruno Nettl, *The Study of Ethnomusicology: Twenty-nine Issues and Concepts* (Urbana: University of Illinois Press, 1983); and Kerman, *Contemplating Music*, 155–181.

74. Helen H. Roberts, *Ancient Hawaiian Music* (Honolulu: Bishop Museum Press, 1926; and Helen H. Roberts, "Hawaiian Music," in Thrum, *Hawaiian Almanac and Annual for 1926* (Honolulu, 1927), 69–80.

75. Marques, "Music in Hawaii Nei," in Thrum, *Hawaiian Almanac and Annual for 1886* (Honolulu, 1887), 51.

76. Ibid., 55.

77. Ibid., 56–60.

78. A. Marques, "Ancient Hawaiian Music," in Thrum, *Hawaiian Almanac and Annual for 1914* (Honolulu, 1915), 103.

79. Kaeppler makes the same point in her historical and critical review of Western studies of Polynesian aesthetic practices, observing "that Polynesians themselves have little place in the analyses, and music appears to exist independently of the people." See Adrienne Kaeppler, "Art and Aesthetics," in *Developments in Polynesian Ethnology*, ed. Alan Howard and Robert Borofsky (Honolulu: University of Hawaii Press, 1989), 227.

80. Trevor Wishart, "Musical Writing, Musical Speaking," in Shepherd, Virden, Vulliamy, and Wishart, *Whose Music?* 125–153.

81. Edward Said, *Orientalism* (New York: Random House, 1978), 67.

Chapter Seven

1. Adrienne L. Kaeppler, "Pacific Festivals," in *Come Mek Me Hol' Yu Han': The Impact of Tourism on Traditional Music* (Jamaica: Jamaica Memory Bank, Institute of Jamaica, 1988), 133.

2. "Stormy Heavens Shake Some at Hula Festival," *Star-Bulletin and Honolulu Advertiser*, April 6, 1986.

3. Stuart Hall, "The Toad in the Garden: Thatcherism among the Theorists," in *Marxism and the Interpretation of Culture*, ed. Cary Nelson and Laurence Grossberg (Urbana: University of Illinois Press,

1988), 35–73. For further discussions of Gramsci's concept of hegemony, see Christine Buci-Glucksmann, "Hegemony and Consent: A Political Strategy," in *Approaches to Gramsci,* ed. Anne Showstack Sassoon (London: Writers and Readers Publishing Cooperative Society, 1982), 116–126; Anne Showstack Sassoon, *Gramsci's Politics,* 2nd ed. (London: Hutchinson, 1987).

4. Robert C. Schmitt, *The Missionary Censuses of Hawaii* (Honolulu: Bernice P. Bishop Museum, 1973), 37. David E. Stannard, *Before the Horror: The Population of Hawai'i on the Eve of Western Contact* (Honolulu: Social Science Research Institute, University of Hawaii, 1989).

5. Caspar Whitney, *Hawaiian America: Something of Its History, Resources, and Prospects* (New York: Harper & Brothers, 1899), 1, 46–47. Whitney's "factual" analysis of "Hawaiian America," a book he dedicated to "Sanford B. Dole, Lorrin A. Thurston, and Benjamin F. Dillingham, Three of Hawaii's Most Loyal and Enterprising Citizens," is an example of the rhetoric of the pro-American forces. For another apologia for the Western assumption of control over the islands, see Stanley D. Porteus, *Calabashes and Kings: An Introduction to Hawaii* (Palo Alto, Calif.: Pacific Books, 1945).

6. Davianna Pomaika'i McGregor, "Perpetuation of the Hawaiian People," in *Ethnicty and Nation-building in the Pacific,* ed. Michael C. Howard (Tokyo: United Nations University, 1989), 83–84.

7. Rod Burgess, "Hawaiian Home Lands Solution," Office of Hawaiian Affairs Newsletter, September 1990, 24. For information on land in Hawai'i and the history and politics of its use, see Eileen Tamura, Cornelia Anguay, and James Shon, eds., *Databook and Atlas: The Shaping of Modern Hawaiian History,* (Honolulu: University of Hawai'i, Curriculum Research and Development Group, 1983).

8. Gavin Daws, *Shoal of Time: A History of the Hawaiian Islands* (Honolulu: University of Hawaii Press, 1968), 293–299. In 1980, the state legislature passed a law giving 20 percent of income from ceded lands to the Office of Hawaiian Affairs. Ceded lands were transferred to Hawai'i when it became a state in 1959. Ceded lands total about 1 million acres and include the Hawaiian Home Lands. In 1989 the state government and the Office of Hawaiian Affairs finally reached agreement on an annual rent of $8.5 million; see "Hawaiians to Get

Millions," *Honolulu Advertiser,* February 9, 1991, A1, A4. In the fall of 1991, a long and detailed article in the *Wall Street Journal* again generated embarrassment for the state and renewed debate at the local level over the mismanagement of Hawaiian Home Lands.

9. McGregor, "Perpetuation of the Hawaiian People," 88–91.

10. Ronald Takaki, *Pau Hana: Plantation Life and Labor in Hawaii, 1835–1920* (Honolulu: University of Hawaii Press, 1983), 140.

11. Ibid., 75–76.

12. Ibid., 66.

13. Ibid., 77.

14. In 1920 there were 109,000 Japanese in the islands, constituting 43 percent of the population. *Haoles* were the next largest group (21 percent), with Hawaiians, Chinese, and Filipinos each making up roughly 10 percent of the population. Robert C. Schmitt, *Historical Statistics of Hawaii* (Honolulu: University Press of Hawaii, 1977), 25.

15. Edward D. Beechert, "The Political Economy of Hawaii and Working Class Consciousness," *Social Process in Hawaii* 31 (1984–1985), 167.

16. For accounts of the political changes in the islands after the war, particularly the rise to power of the local Democratic party and the constituencies of that party, see George Cooper and Gavan Daws, *Land and Power in Hawai'i: The Democratic Years* (Honolulu: Benchmark Books, 1985); and Tom Coffman, *To Catch a Wave; A Case Study of Hawaii's New Politics,* 2nd ed. (Honolulu: University Press of Hawaii, 1973).

17. DeSoto Brown, *Hawaii Recalls: Selling Romance to America: Nostalgic Images of the Hawaiian Islands, 1920–1950* (Honolulu: Editions Limited, 1982).

18. Elizabeth Tatar, *Strains of Change: The Impact of Tourism on Hawaiian Music,* Special Publication no. 78 (Honolulu: Bernice P. Bishop Museum, 1987).

19. Raymond Williams, *The Sociology of Culture* (New York: Schocken Books, 1981), 104.

20. Ron Jacobs, "Peter Moon: Interview," *Honolulu: The Paradise of the Pacific* 25, no. 4 (October 1990): 46–54.

21. The local music industry association that started in 1978, Nā Hōkū Hanohano (The Stars of Distinction), tries to keep track of the

production of local recordings on an annual basis. All such recordings are eligible for the annual awards that are announced at a Grammy-type gala function each spring.

22. For additional discussions of the recording industry in Hawai'i, see Elizabeth Bentzel Buck, "The Hawaii Music Industry," *Social Process in Hawaii* 31 (1984–85): 137–153; Elizabeth Bentzel Buck, "A Brief History of Contemporary Music Production in Hawai'i," in *Whose Master's Voice?* ed. Alison Ewbank and Fouli Papageorgiou (Westport, Conn.: Greenwood Press, 1992); Jerry Hopkins, "Record Industry in Hawaii," in *Hawaiian Music and Musicians: An Illustrated History*, ed. George S. Kanahele (Honolulu: University Press of Hawaii, 1979), 325–334.

23. Buck, "Hawaii Music Industry," 142–145.

24. Kit Smith, "Big Business, Big Changes," *Honolulu Star-Bulletin and Advertiser*, December 31, 1989, A8; Janice Otaguro, "Tourists: Can't Live with 'Em; Can't Live without 'Em," *Honolulu* 26, no. 2 (August 1991): 43–45, 147–152.

25. Jean Baudrillard, *For a Critique of the Political Economy of the Sign*, trans. Charles Levin (St Louis: Telos Press, 1981).

26. "Hawaii's Labor Shortage," *Economic Indicators* (Honolulu: Research Department, First Hawaiian Bank, July/August 1990).

27. The theme of *aloha* as an economic resource was an important topic of discussion at the 1984 "Congress" on tourism. See Hawaii, Governor's Tourism Congress, *Proceedings*, December 10–11, 1984 (Honolulu: Department of Planning and Economic Development, 1985). Four years later, the 1988 Governor's Congress on Hawaii's International Role reflected growing concern over excessive dependence on tourism and the fragility of the islands' "quality of life." See Hawaii, Governor's Congress on Hawaii's International Role, *Report* (Honolulu, December 6–7, 1988).

28. Smith, "Big Business, Big Changes," A8.

29. Theoretical discussions on subcultures and their relationship with the hegemonic dominant culture are found in the following: John Clarke, Stuart Hall, Tony Jefferson, and Brian Roberts, "Subcultures, Cultures and Class: A Theoretical Overview," in *Resistance through Rituals: Youth Subcultures in Post-War Britain*, ed. Stuart Hall and Tony Jefferson (London: Hutchinson, 1976), 9–79; Raymond

Williams, *Marxism and Literature* (Oxford, England: Oxford University Press, 1977). Bakhtin's discussion of counterdiscourses that resist the centripetal pull of the dominant culture is relevant to Hawai'i. See Mikhail M. Bakhtin, *The Dialogic Imagination: Four Essays by M. M. Bakhtin*, ed. Michael Holquist and trans. Caryl Emerson and Michael Holquist (Austin: University of Texas Press, 1981).

30. According to some critics of OHA such as Mililani Trask, an attorney, and her sister, Haunani-Kay Trask, who is director of the University of Hawaii's Hawaiian Studies Program, the establishment of OHA was little more than another symbolic gesture designed to appease Hawaiians and has had the effect of defusing the political energy of the Hawaiian movement. OHA is semi-autonomous in that its trustees are elected by Hawaiians. However, it is a creation of the state and restricted in what it is able to do.

31. The 1990 U.S. census shows 12.5 percent of the state's population as Hawaiian, a slight increase over the 12 percent of 1980. See State of Hawaii, Department of Business, Economic Development and Tourism, *State of Hawaii Data Book* (1990), rev.

32. U.S. Native Hawaiians Study Commission, *Report on the Culture, Needs and Concerns of Native Hawaiians Pursuant to Public Law 96–565, Title III* (Washington, D.C.: The Commission, 1983).

33. "Ka Lāhui Hawai'i Challenges OHA in Quest for Hawaiian Sovereignty," *Ka Wai Ola O OHA* 8, no. 9 (*Kapakemapa*) (September 1991). OHA also favors sovereignty under a "nation within a nation" model. For an overview of the different groups formed since the 1970s to fight for Hawaiian rights, see McGregor, "Perpetuation of the Hawaiian People," 91–95. Approximately 45–50 different Hawaiian groups have formed a sovereignty coalition called *Hui Na'auao*. Some, such as the Institute for the Advancement of Hawaiian Affairs, favor total independence from the United States for the islands.

34. See Stuart Hall, "The Rediscovery of 'Ideology': Return of the Repressed in Media Studies," in *Culture, Society and Media*, ed. Michael Gurevitch, Tony Bennett, James Curan, and Janet Woollacott (London: Methuen, 1982), 72.

35. For a discussion of the geothermal issue, see Joan Conrow, "Geothermal: Pele's Last Stand?" *Honolulu* 24 no. 12 (June 1990).

36. Suzanne Tswei, "Activists Call for Hawaiian Sovereignty at Meeting," *Honolulu Advertiser*, December 4, 1988.

37. "15th Na Hoku Hanohano: The Winners Are . . ." *Honolulu Star Bulletin*, April 6, 1992, D6).

38. Roland Barthes, "Theory of the Text," in *Untying the Text: A Post-Structuralist Reader*, ed. Robert Young (Boston: Routledge and Kegan Paul, 1981).

Glossary

I have used Hawaiian spellings except in quotes, titles, or names of entities, where I have followed the original source regarding macrons and glottal stops. Definitions and spellings are based on Mary Kawena Pukui and Samuel H. Elbert, *Hawaiian Dictionary*, rev. and enlarged ed. (Honolulu: University of Hawaii Press, 1986). *Hula* and chant terms are based on Betty Tatar, *Nineteenth Century Hawaiian Chant*, Pacific Anthropological Records No. 33 (Honolulu: Department of Anthropology, Bernice P. Bishop Museum, 1982). I have used Hawai'i throughout, unless a quote or the name of an entity does not use the glottal stop.

ahupua'a:	Traditional land division, usually extending from the uplands to the sea.
'āina:	Land.
ali'i:	A chief, royalty.
ali'i'aimoku:	The paramount chief of a district.
ali'i nui:	A high chief.
haku mele:	A poet, composer of chant, often a priest.
hālau:	A school or schools, as for *hula* instruction.
haole:	A Caucasian: formerly used for any foreigner.
hapa haole:	Part-Caucasian or part-Western.
hapa haole music:	Popular music of the twentieth century, usually with a few Hawaiian words or about Hawai'i.
heiau:	Hawaiian place of worship: a shrine or temple.

hīmeni:	Hymn: songs based on Western music forms.
huhū:	Angry, scolding.
hula:	Hawaiian dance. There are many types of *hula*.
hula 'auana:	Modern *hula*, as opposed to *hula kahiko*.
hula inoa:	*Hula* accompanying a chant praising an *ali'i*.
hula kahiko:	Traditional *hula*. The term emerged in the twentieth century to distinguish pre-European chant and *hula* from Western-influenced songs and *hula*.
hula ku'i:	Part-Western music and dance styles that evolved in the late nineteenth century; *ku'i* means "to combine."
hula ma'i:	*Hula* in honor of chief's genitals and fertility and hence his *mana*.
hula pahu:	Traditional *hula* accompanied by a *pahu*, a wooden sharkskin drum, considered sacred because the drum was used in *heiau* rituals.
kahuna:	A priest; an expert in any profession; *kāhuna* is plural.
kahuna pule:	A priest specialized in praying.
kaona:	Hidden or layered meanings highly valued in Hawaiian chant.
kapu:	Sacred, forbidden; prohibitions, rules.
kapu ā moe:	Prostration *kapu*.
kapu ā noho:	Sitting *kapu*.
kauwā:	Slaves, outcasts.
konohiki:	The headman of a land division under a chief.

kuleana:	Piece of land, responsibility.
kumu hula:	A *hula* teacher.
kupuna:	A grandparent; one of the older generation; *kūpuna* is plural.
lāhui:	Race, nation.
lei:	A flower wreath worn around the neck.
luakini heiau:	A large *heiau* where human sacrifices were offered.
lū'au:	A Hawaiian feast; term used this way since the 1850s.
Māhele:	Land division of 1848.
maka'āinana:	A commoner; people in general.
makahiki:	Annual festival in the fall.
mana:	Spiritual power; divinely powerful.
mele:	Chant, song, poem.
mele hula:	Chanting accompanied by *hula.*
mele inoa:	Name chant.
mele oli:	Chanting unaccompanied by *hula.*
mele pahu:	Chant to the beat of the *pahu* drum.
mō'ī:	King, ruler; first used in print in 1832.
mo'ōlelo:	Story, history, myth.
mu'umu'u:	A loose dress.
noa:	Freed of tabu, released from restrictions.
'ohana:	Family or extended family.
'ōlelo:	Language, speech, words; to speak.
oli:	Chant that is not accompanied by *hula.*
'ōpū:	Stomach.
palapala:	Writing or document of any kind.
poi:	Food made from cooked and pounded *taro.*
pono:	Goodness, well-being, righteousness.

tapa:	Cloth made from bark; also *kapa.*
taro:	A plant from which *poi* is made.
tī:	A plant with long leaves used for many things, including skirts for *hula;* also *kī.*
tūtū wāhine:	Grandmothers.
'ukulele:	Ukulele.

Index